1

Kittel & Graf

History of the U-Boot

ISBN 978-2-37297-1768

Copyright 2015
Edizioni R.E.I.
www.edizionirei.com
info@edizionirei.com

Kittel & Graf

HISTORY OF THE U-BOOT

Edizioni R.E.I.

Index

U-Boot

U-Boot is the German term to refer broadly to submarines, and is short for Unterseeboot, literally "submarine boat".
The term is used in other languages as a synonym of the boats used submarines from the German Navy during the First and Second World War, although it is often written as "anglicized" U-Boat. The objectives of the U-boat campaigns in both wars were the convoys carrying supplies from the US to Europe. The term U-Boot, followed by a number, such as U-Boot 47 indicates a specific vessel, while U-Boot Type II a particular class; the only U-Boot that can be considered true submarines, and not submarines, are those that belong to the Type XXI and Type XXIII. During the Second World War, the attacks of the U-boats were the main component of the Battle of the North Eastern, which lasted until the end of the war.
During the early stages of the war and immediately after the entry of the United States, the U-boats were extremely effective in the destruction of merchant allies. Improvements in tactical convoys, sonar, the depth charges, the deciphering of the Enigma code used by the Germans and the range of escort aircraft served to turn the fate against the U-boats. At the end of the U-boat fleet suffered extremely heavy losses, losing 789 units (three British submarines captured) of 1,157 (of which 25 Allied captured) and about 30,000 sailors on a total of 50,000. Germany also had 700 small submarines. It should be remembered the help of Italian submarines, which helped with 32 units and 109 ships sunk the German ally. The German U-boats and Japanese submarines and Italian sank around 2,828 Allied ships, for a total of about 15 million tons. Between 1939 and 1942 the U-boats also bombed the oil fields of Florida and Americans of many coastal areas causing extensive damage; when the British found a way to decipher Enigma allies were able to predict the movements, yet the Germans did not interrupt the use of U-boats in the Atlantic.
Winston Churchill, Prime Minister of the United Kingdom for much of the war, seems to have said: "The only thing that really frightened me during the war was the U-boat threat."

During World War II, the Kriegsmarine (German Navy) produced different types of U-boats, as the technology improved:

- Submarines Germans built: 1,162
- Submarines Germans sunk: 784
- 40,000 men employed on board
- 28,000 sailors of U-Boot died over 5,000 taken prisoner
- Sinking Allied ships: 2,828 (total data of the whole war, were aided by more than 30 Italian submarines and Japanese ones)
- Often bombed the oil fields of Florida, causing extensive damage.
- Caused about 30,000 deaths among the allied navies, which largely sailors were civilians, but they knew the risk they were facing.

At the end of hostilities 45 boats were still at sea, of these: 23 are handed over to the British, three in the United States, two in Argentina, two were self-sunk, one ended up stranded on the coasts of the Dutch, the remainder ended up in Norwegian ports and Kiel or in the port of Wihelmshaven.

Kriegsmarine

The Kriegsmarine (German Navy) was the name of the German Navy during World War II, heir to the Kaiserliche Marine. The Treaty of Versailles had imposed strict limits to the German Navy and had prohibited the design and construction of submarines, aircraft carriers, naval aircraft and coastal artillery heavy; the displacement of the new ships could not exceed 10,000 tons. But on June 18, 1935 was signed the Anglo-German Naval Treaty, which, while limiting the strength of the German navy to 35% of the English one, allowed Germany to have submarines and other vessels that the Treaty of Versailles had forbidden. In 1937 thus began an ambitious plan for shipbuilding (Z plane) and September 1939 the German Navy had two old battleships, 2 battle cruisers, 3 pocket battleships, two heavy cruisers, 6 light cruisers, 22 destroyers, 20 torpedo boats 59 and U-Boot. During the conflict entered service battleships Tirpitz and Bismarck, the heavy cruiser Prinz Eugen and another 15 destroyers. The Kriegsmarine was divided into three fundamental branches under the command of Admiral Erich Raeder. Battleships depended directly dall'Oberkommando der Marine (OKM) and then by the commanders of the group (Gruppenkommandos).

The flotillas of minesweepers, patrol ships, ships for coastal defense and ships auxiliary were at the controls of the Section of ship safety. The third branch, which would become the worst threat to the Allies at sea, was the command submarines Karl Doenitz. Unlike most other marine, the Kriegsmarine had no airplanes in own; all'OKM (Oberkommando der Marine), was awarded a general aviation, which was to provide marine transportation it needed. The Führer der Marineluftstreitkräfte was Major General Hans Geisler.

In 1940 Admiral Karl Doenitz declared that "the U-boats alone could win the war"; In fact, the submarine was the major obstacle to the success of the Allies: for the second time in 25 years, Germany was able to cut the maritime communications of the Allies.

The weapon of the U-boats was organized under the command of Doenitz, who was Führer der Unterseeboote (commander of submarines). In 1939 a total of 55 submarines was divided into flotillas, each with a number of U-boats ranging from 5 to 8, some of which received the name of the heroes of the U-boats of World War I. In 1941 began the Rudeltaktik (tactical group) or a pack of wolves tactics: groups of 15 to 20 U-boats patrolled the routes in the vicinity of Great Britain; when a convoy was sighted, was being chased by a submarine that broadcast radio for the position, course and composition to the headquarters of Doenitz, with whom he kept in connection, as long as other submarines had not received their orders and made contact . Then the U-boats attacked simultaneously, but independently, to report later on the result of their action to Doenitz, who gave orders for a further attack or a new patrol. By adopting this tactic tonnage sunk steadily increased and 1942 proved to be the most profitable year: the U-boats sank 1,160 ships, for a total of about 6.3 million tons. Gradually, however, the improvement of the techniques allied assault and the use of long-range airplanes, aircraft carriers and escort ships equipped with radar began to yield results: between April and May 1943 the tonnage sunk by German submarines began to decrease, while their losses increased. This is in part due to the ability of allied commands to decipher the secret codes of the German command.

It is in this period that the commands allies manage to get hold of the machine used by the Germans to crack the code "Enigma". The losses among the German submarines go up from 13 to 30% in May; then the U-boats survivors, about 16, were withdrawn from the North Atlantic. Half of 1943 was a turning point in the Battle of the Atlantic; the Allied offensive began to become more and more consistent, while the German attempt to posit brake came too late. The German submarines, throughout the world conflict, caused the loss of 175 warships and 2,603 Allied ships cargo for a total of 14 million tons.

More than 39,000 officers and sailors saw service in the German submarines and 32,000 were killed in action, the highest proportion of all other forces during the war.

Type I

The U-Boot Type IA (German U-Boot Typ IA) was the first class of U-Boot suited to ocean navigation and designed to operate at a great distance.
For this reason were launched after the U-Boot Type II whose use short range made them priority.
Given a little project failed due to poor handling and long immersion time, they were made only two specimens (U-25 and U-26), which entered service in early 1936 Kriegsmarine.
Despite the limited success, the design of Type IA was the basis of subsequent projects of U-Boot, especially for classes Type VII and Type IX.
The two units were mainly used for training and as a tool of Nazi propaganda until 1939, when - with the start of World War II - took part, albeit briefly, the so-called Battle of the Atlantic (1939-1945).
In this long naval conflict, the action of U-Boot was designed mainly to isolate the blocking supplies from England, away freighter, mainly from North America.

- Displacement: 862 tons surfaced, 983 tons submerged
- Length: 72.39 meters
- Width: 6.21 meters
- Draft: 4.30 meters
- Operating depth: 150 meters (depth of implosion: 200 meters)
- Propulsion: 2 diesel engines 8-cylinder 1,540 hp each, two electric motors BBC 500 hp
- Maximum power: 3,080 hp in emergence (Diesel), 1000 CV in diving (electric motor)
- Speed emersion: 18.6 knots
- Speed immersion: 8.3 knots
- Dive time: 30 seconds
- Diesel oil: 96 tons
- Batteries: 124 elements 36MAK 740 (9260 amps)
- Autonomy in surfacing: 7.900 nautical miles at 10 knots, nautical 6700 miles at 12 knots

- Autonomy in dive 78 nautical miles at 4 knots
- Crew: 43 men (4 officers and 39 crew members)
- Armament: 6 torpedo tubes (4 forward and 2 aft) 14 torpedoes G7E
- Mine: 28 anti-ship mines TMA
- Cannons: 1 105 mm gun, one anti-aircraft gun from 20 mm

Launched February 14, 1936, entered service April 6 of that year.

The U-25, commanded by Viktor Schutze, participated in five missions between October 1939 and August 1940, sinking six British merchant and an escort ship, the HMS British armed merchant Scotstoun. Between April and May of 1940, the unit was used in the North Sea and at the western coast of Norway as part of Operation Weserübung.

Operation Weserübung is the definition given in the German military in the early stages of the invasion of Norway and Denmark took place April 9, 1940.

The military objective of the operation was the occupation of the Norwegian ports to prevent a possible block of the same by England and the German war industry to ensure the supply of iron ore mined in Kiruna (Sweden) came in Narvik .

U 25 in navigation

Planners of the operation, commanded by General Nikolaus von Falkenhorst, the occupation of Denmark, as transit alternative for the material, it seemed inevitable. The Lebensborn project is strongly connected to this military operation that enabled the start of the German occupation of Scandinavia.

To August 3, 1940 was the last known position of the U-Boot that was later declared missing.

The most accepted is that reconstruction is sunk, along with the entire crew, on the high seas to the north of the Dutch city of Terschelling, at approximately 54°14'N and 5°7'W, for the collision with a mine naval.

Remain unclear, however, the dynamics of the sinking and when the collision occurred with its own mine (the unit had to perform an operation of deployment of anti-ship mines) or through a minefield that had been laid out in that area by British destroyers August 3rd.

U-26

Launched on March 14, 1936, entered service on 11 May of that year.

The U-26 participated in seven missions, between the end of August 1939 and June 1940, sinking around eleven ships and damaging two. In the last mission attacked the Allied convoy OA-175 sinking, the same day, three transport ships (Frangoula B Goulandris, Merkur and Belmoira) and damaging one (the freighter Zarian English).

Intercepted, after the attack, two enemy ships, sloop of war HMS Rochester and the corvette HMS Gladiolus, was hit by it with depth charges. The German submarine, unable to keep the dive because of the damage suffered, he was forced to emerge again to be bombed by a squadron of Short S.25 Sunderland RAF.

Now condemned, the U-26 was abandoned and sank on 1 July 1940, at 48°03'N and 11°30'W off the southwest coast of Ireland. The entire crew (48 men) was rescued and taken prisoner by the HMS Rochester.

Type II

Dubbed Einbaum (dugout canoe) by their crews, the U-boats were the first type II class submarines built for the Kriegsmarine after the First World War. While the old prototype I (who would eventually evolved in U-Boat from great distances IX) was designed as a submarine fleet, the type II was designed as a short-range coastal vessel, especially for defensive use.
The boat prototype entered service with Merivoimat, the Finnish Navy, and took the name of Vesikko, being used against the Soviet naval forces in the Baltic during the naval operations in the Winter War.
Because of their limited range and relatively weak armament (three torpedo tubes and a machine gun), after 1940 the U-Boat type II were used mainly for training.
However 6 models II-B were disassembled and transported by barge, road and rail to the port of Constanza on the Black Sea, where they acted against the Soviet navy.
A total of 50 units of Type II were built during the war.

Type II-A

The original variant, of which 6 were produced specimens (U1 to U6) all in 1935.

The Type II-A had a single hull with internal ballast tanks; than the other variants had a smaller bridge and could carry torpedoes G7a and torpedo G7E as mines TMA.

There was only one periscope in the turret.

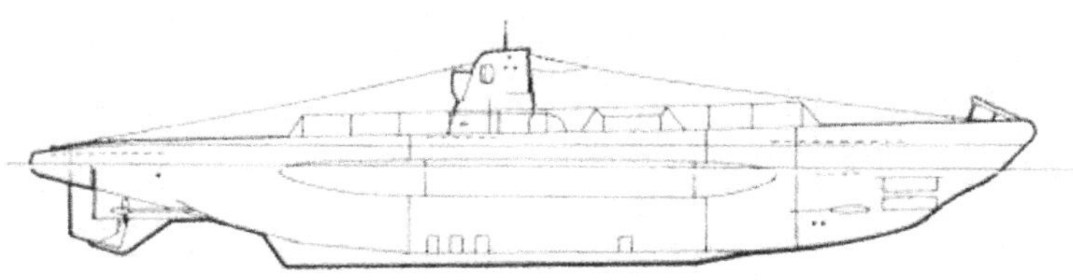

- Displacement: 254 tons (surfaced), 303 tons (submerged)
- Length: 40.90 meters
- Width: 4.08 meters
- Draft: 3.83 meters
- Height: 8.60 meters
- Maximum power: 700 hp (surfaced), 360 hp (submerged)
- Gas oil: 12 tons
- Propulsion: two diesel engines 6-cylinder 700 hp each, two electric motors SSW 300 kW
- Maximum speed: 13 knots (surfaced), 6.9 knots (submerged)
- Autonomy: 1,050 nautical miles (at 12 knots surfaced), 1,600 miles nautical (8 knots surfaced), 35 nautical miles (4 knots submerged)
- Depth: 100 meters (operational), 150 meters (maximum)
- Immersion time: 35 seconds
- Torpedo tubes: 3 forward, no one aft
- Refills: 5
- Mine: 18 TMA
- Cannons: 1 20mm cannon

- Crew: 25 men (3 officers and 22 crew members

List of boats Type IIA:
- U-1
- U-2
- U-3
- U-4
- U-5
- U-6

Tipo II-B

Launched for the first time in 1935, the Type II-B represented an attempt to increase the autonomy of the series type II.
The hull was increased in length to accommodate a reservoir of additional fuel under the control room. The immersion time was improved to 30 seconds.
20 units built so designated:
- from U-7 to U-12
- from U-13 to U-16
- from U-17 to U-24
- from U-120 to U-121

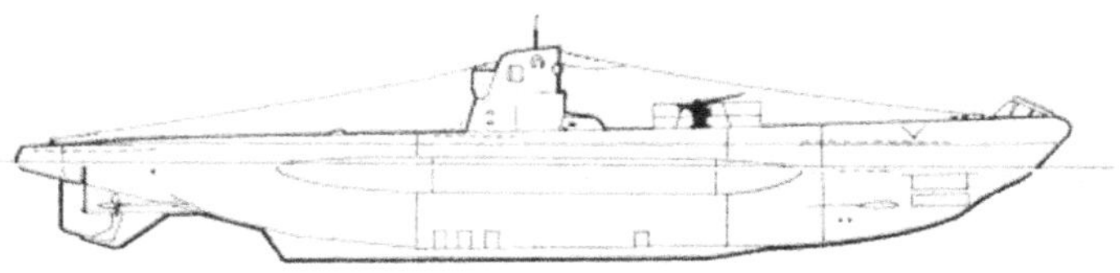

- Displacement: 279 tons (surfaced), 329 tons (submerged)
- Length: 42.7 meters
- Width: 4.1 meters
- Draft: 3.9 meters
- Maximum speed: 13 knots (surfaced), 7 knots (submerged)
- Gas oil 21 tons
- Propulsion: two diesel engines 6-cylinder 700 hp each, two electric motors SSW 300 kW
- Batteries: 62 elements 36 MAK 580 to 7160 amps or 62 elements 44 MAL 570 to 8380 amperes
- Autonomy: 3900 miles nautical (8 knots surfaced) 1,800 nautical miles (at 12 knots surfaced), 43 nautical miles (4 knots submerged)
- Depth: 100 meters (operational), 150 meters (maximum)
- Torpedo tubes: 3 forward, no one at the stern
- Refills: 5
- Cannons: 1 of 20 mm cannon
- Crew: 25 men (3 officers and 22 crew members).

Type II-C

The type II-C was a stretched version of the Type II-B, which enabled a further increase in the radius of action and space for the equipment necessary with the addition of two compartments at midships and diesel tanks under the room control, total operating range of 1,900 nautical miles at 12 knots surfaced.
8 units built so designated: from U-56 to U-63.
A pair of type II-C were the first U-boats to be equipped with devices operating schnorchel that allowed them to move thanks to diesel engines during diving, in addition to being provided with a second periscope. This variant was launched for the first time in 1938.

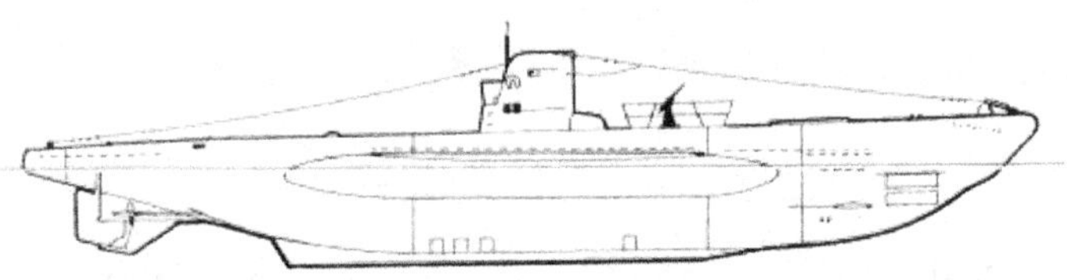

- Displacement: 291 tons (surfaced), 341 tons (submerged)
- Length: 43.9 meters
- Width: 4.1 meters
- Draft: 3.8 meters
- Gas oil 23 tons
- Maximum speed: 12 knots (surfaced), 7 knots (submerged)
- Propulsion: two diesel engines 6-cylinder 700 hp each, two electric motors SSW 300 kW
- Autonomy: 4.200 nautical miles (8 knots surfaced), 1900 miles nautical (12 knots surfaced), 42 nautical miles (4 knots submerged)
- Depth: 100 meters (operational), 150 meters (maximum)
- Torpedo tubes: 3 forward, no one at the stern
- Refills: 5 bow
- Cannons: 1 20mm cannon
- Crew: 25 men (3 officers and 22 crew members.

Type II-D

This final variant of the Type II had extra fuel tanks additional "saddle" mounted on the sides of the outer hull, similar to those used on the U-Boot Type VII. This allowed to bring autonomy 3,450 nautical miles to 12 miles in surfacing giving it a range sufficient to operate close to the islands of Great Britain.
16 units built so designated: U-137 to U-152.
A further development was the propellers with nozzles Kurt, aimed at improving the efficiency of propulsion.
Launched the first time in 1940, the Type II-D saw active service only for a short period, since strong was the need for vessels of training for new recruits; by 1941 all of these models were then relegated to training duties.

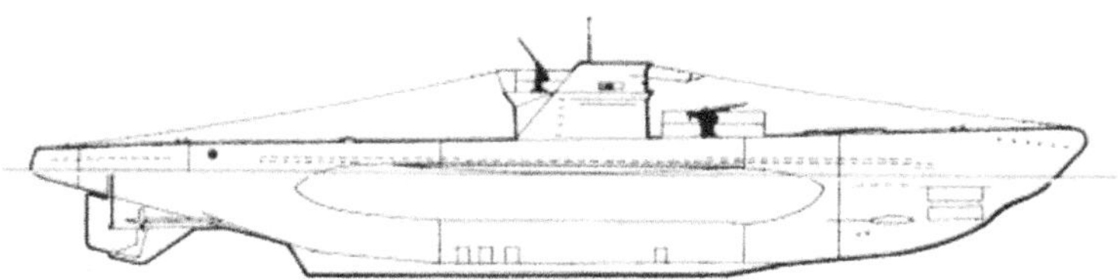

- Displacement: 314 tons (surfaced), 364 tons (submerged)
- Length: 44.0 meters
- Width: 5.0 meters
- Draft: 3.9 meters
- Gas oil 38 tons
- Propulsion: two diesel engines 6-cylinder 700 hp each, two electric motors SSW 300 kW
- Batteries: 62 elements 36 MAK 580 to 7160 amps or 62 elements 44 MAL 570 to 8380 amperes
- Maximum speed: 13 (surfaced), 7.9 knots (submerged)
- Autonomy: 3450 miles nautical (12 knots surfaced), 56 nautical miles (4 knots submerged)
- Depth: 125 meters (operational), 175 meters (maximum)
- Immersion time: 25 seconds
- Torpedo tubes: 3 forward, no one at the stern
- Refills: 5

- Cannons: 1 gun from 20 mm anti-aircraft
- Crew: 26 men (3 officers and 23 crew members).

Type V

The U-Boat Type V was a type of mini submarine experimental from 76 tons designed by Hellmuth Walter that used the hydrogen peroxide to drive the turbine.
It was built just a boat: the V-80.
The V-80 was the first boat Walter. It was built by F. Krupp Germaniawerft in Kiel in 1939-1940 and was powered by a turbine (20,000 rpm). The crew consisted of four people and the boat was unarmed since it was built exclusively for research purposes. V-80 was used for various tests and tapped all of the records in immersion speed as the vessel was able to reach 28 knots. The V80 was taken out of service at the end of 1942, and sunk in Hela in March 1945.

Type VII

The U-Boot Type VII is a German submarine Atlantic class U-Boot, active in World War II. It is characterized by a good handling and a quick immersion.

The design of the Type VII was chosen by discarding the study of the previous Type IA, this especially for the amount less than that allowed the production of more U-boats within the limits of displacement imposed by the Treaty of Peace signed by Germany at the end of the War world.

The project was very apt and formed the backbone of the U-boat fleet with more than 700 submarines of all subtypes completed, by far the type of U-Boot larger.

10 units built so designated: from U-27 to U-32 built in shipyards Deschimag in Bremen and from U-33 to U-36 built in shipyards Germaniawerft in Kiel.

The Royal Navy was to be equipped with nine of these boats (U428, U746, U747, U429, U748, U430, U749, U750 and U1161, renamed the order S1 to S9) that would have made up the S-Class in exchange for 9 boats Italian allocated BETASOM (to be converted to the transport of rare metals and valuable products for the war industry and from the Far East), but the Armistice of Cassibile obviously produced a cancellation of delivery. The armistice of Cassibile (also called Armistice short), was an agreement signed secretly in the town of Cassibile, on 3 September 1943, and is the act by which the Kingdom of Italy ceased hostilities against the Anglo-American forces allied, as part of World War II. In fact it was not at all an armistice, but a true unconditional surrender.

Since this act established its entry into force from the moment of its public announcement, it is commonly referred to as "September 8", when, at 18:30, was announced first on Radio Algiers by General Dwight Eisenhower and, just over an hour later, at 19:42, confirmed by the proclamation of Marshal Pietro Badoglio transmitted by the microphones EIAR (Italian Agency for radio programs). He achieved many successes, including the violation of Scapa Flow, the basis of " home fleet "British.

U-Boot Type VII C/41

- Displacement: 626 tons (surfaced), 745 tons (submerged)
- Length: 64.51 meters
- Width: 5.85 meters
- Draft: 4.37 meters
- Maximum speed: 17.2 knots (surfaced), 8 knots (submerged)
- Propulsion: 2 diesel engines from 2,320 hp, two electric motors of 750 hp (560 kW)
- Autonomy: 6,200 miles nautical (10 knots surfaced), 73 nautical miles (4 knots submerged)
- Depth: 100 meters (operational), 200 meters (maximum)
- Immersion time: 50 seconds
- Torpedo tubes: 4 forward, 1 aft
- Refills: 11
- Cannons: 1 naval cannon 88 mm C / 35, 1 20-mm anti-aircraft gun. À since 1944 two 37 mm cannons Flak
- Crew: 4 officers and 44 to 56 crew members.

Type VII-B

The original variant of the Type VII had a launch tube that was rear-mounted externally. This embarrassing solution was then corrected in Type VII-B, which was equipped with a room of stern launch and space for a refill for the single launch tube aft.
24 units built so designated:
- From U-45 to U-55 built in shipyards in Kiel Germaniawerft
- From U-73 to U-76 built in shipyards Vegesacker Werft in Vegesack
- From U-83 to U-87 built-in yards Flender Werft in Lübeck
- From U-99 to U-102 built in shipyards in Kiel Germaniawerft

The Type VII-B was also equipped with watertight compartments on the upper deck that were used for storing additional refills torpedo.
The Type VII-B was also provided with additional autonomy and more speed than the original variant, allowing To advance further into the Atlantic Ocean. It was launched in 1938.
In total 24 were commissioned U-Boot Type VII-B.

- Displacement: 753 tons (surfaced), 857 tons (submerged)
- Length: 66.5 meters
- Width: 6.2 meters
- Draft: 4.7 meters
- Maximum speed: 17.2 knots (surfaced), 8 knots (submerged)
- Propulsion: 2 diesel engines MAN 6-cylinder 1,160 hp or two diesel engines Germaniawerft F46 6-cylinder 1,400 hp, two electric motors BBC GG UB 720/8 375 hp or 2 electric motors AEG OJ 460 / 8-276 375 hp
- Autonomy: 6.500 nautical miles (at 12 knots surfaced), 90 nautical miles (4 knots submerged)
- Depth: 150 meters (operational), 225 meters (maximum)

- Dive time: 30 seconds
- torpedo tubes: 4 forward, 1 aft
- Refills: 14
- Cannons: 1 naval cannon C / 35 to 88 mm, 20 mm machine gun 1 C30. Starting from 1944, one 37 mm cannon and four machine guns twin 20mm Flak
- Crew: 4 officers and 40 to 56 crew members

Type VII-C

The Type VII-C is by far the most numerous variant of any U-boats ever built, with 577 units completed at the end of the War. The length was increased compared to that of VII-B, but it was not the power of engines, leading to a slight reduction in performance in immersion.

654 units built so designated:
- by U-69 to U-72
- by U-77 to U-82
- by U-88 to U-92
- by U-93 to U-98
- by U-132 to U-136
- by U-201 to U-212
- by U-221 to U-232
- by U-235 to U-250
- by U-251 to U-299
- by U-301 to U-327
- by U-331 to U-350
- by U-351 to U-370
- by U-371 to U-394
- by U-396 to U-400
- by U-401 to U-430
- by U-431 to U-450
- by U-451 to U-458
- by U-465 to U-486
- by U-551 to U-650
- by U-651 to U-683
- by U-701 to U-722
- by U-731 to U-750
- by U-751 to U-768
- by U-771 to U-779
- by U-821 to U-822
- by U-825 to U-828
- U-901
- by U-903 to U-904
- by U-905 to U-908

- by U-921 to U-930
- by U-951 to U-1005
- by U-1007 to U-1010
- by U-1013 to U-1025
- by U-1051 to U-1058
- by U-1063 to U-1065
- by U-1101 to U-1110
- by U-1131 to U-1132
- by U-1161 to U-1169
- by U-1171 to U-1172
- by U-1191 to U-1210
- by U-1271 to U-1278
- by U-1280 to U-1290
- by U-1301 to U-1307

Launched the first time in 1940, the units of this type formed the backbone of the forces U-boats used in the Battle of the Atlantic.

- Displacement: 761 tons (surfaced), 865 tons (submerged)
- Length: 67.1 meters
- Width: 6.2 meters
- Draft: 4.8 meters
- Maximum speed: 17.2 knots (surfaced), 7.6 knots (submerged)
- Autonomy: 6.500 nautical miles (at 12 knots surfaced), 80 nautical miles (4 knots submerged)
- Propulsion: 2 diesel engines M6V 40/46 6-cylinder in-line 1400 hp, two electric motors AEG OJ 460 / 8-276 375 hp or two electric motors BBC GG UB 720/8 375 hp or two electric motors Garbe Lahmeyer RP 137 / c by two electric motors or Siemens-Schuckert GU 343 / 38-8 375 hp
- Depth: 150 meters (operational), 235 meters (maximum)
- Immersion time: 27 seconds
- Torpedo tubes: 4 forward, 1 aft
- Refills: 14

- Cannons: 1 naval gun SK C / 35 to 88 mm, 1 anti-aircraft cannon C30 20 mm, 26 or 29 antipersonnel mines MTA MTB.
- Crew: 4 officers and 44 to 56 crew members

Type VII-C/41

Faced with the increased efforts anti-submarine Allies, it was decided that there could be room for improvement in the design of the Type VII-C. Increases in the thickness of the hull under pressure in this variant allowed to descend to depths greater and a new design of the bow improved seaworthiness.
In total 88 were commissioned U-Boot Type VII-C/41.
In order to increase the depth, all non-essential equipment have been removed while others have been replaced with new lighter materials. The weight saving has been used to increase the thickness of the hull from 18.5 mm to 21 mm, which has increased the maximum depth of up to 250 meters.

- Displacement: 759 tons (surfaced), 860 tons (submerged)
- Length: 67.2 meters
- Width: 6.2 meters
- Draft: 4.8 meters
- Maximum speed: 17 knots (surfaced), 7.6 knots (submerged)
- Propulsion: 2 diesel engines from 2,320 hp, two electric motors of 750 hp
- Autonomy: 6.500 nautical miles (at 12 knots surfaced), 80 nautical miles (4 knots submerged)
- Depth: 170 meters (operational), 275 meters (maximum)
- Immersion time: 25 seconds
- Torpedo tubes: 4 forward, 1 aft
- Refills: 6
- Cannons: 1 88 mm naval gun, one 20 mm anti-aircraft
- The 88mm gun was omitted, on the other hand was strengthened anti-aircraft component with different combinations; usually two pairs of 20 mm and widened WINTER GARDEN could find a place quadrinata 20mm FlaK 38, or, as happened later with a deadly 3.7 cm FlaK M42U single-tube.
- Crew: 44 men.

Type VII-C/42

A further variant, the Type VII-C/42 was planned, but few specimens were built since the priorities of construction were concentrated on U-Boot again conception Type XXI.
Launched for the first time in 1943, this was the last major variant produced the Type VII.
This project would house an additional compressor, increasing the efficiency of the engine and the autonomy to 10,000 nautical miles. However, the most significant improvement of this project was for the material of the shell quality steel armored. With the expected increase in thickness of 28 mm, the maximum depth was increased to 350 meters.

- Displacement: 999 tons (surfaced), 1,099 tons (submerged)
- Length: 68.7 meters
- Width: 6.7 meters
- Draft: 5.1 meters
- Oil: 159 tons
- Maximum speed: 18.6 knots (surfaced), 8.2 knots (submerged)
- Propulsion: 2 diesel engines M6V 40/46 inline 6-cylinder 1,400 hp, two electric motors of 375 hp
- Batteries: 124 Elementis 27 MAK 740 (6940 Amps) or 124 elements 27 MAK 800 (8,480 amperes) or 124 elements 33 MAL 800 (9160 Amps)
- Autonomy: 10.000 nautical miles (at 12 knots surfaced), 80 nautical miles (4 knots submerged)
- Depth: 250 meters (operational), 350 meters (maximum)
- Immersion time: 27 seconds
- Torpedo tubes: 4 forward, 1 aft
- Refills: 16
- Cannons: 1 gun quadruple 20mm, 1 double cannon 20mm
- Crew: 45 men

Type VII-C/43

Another variant, remained on paper, similar to the VII-C/42 but designed to have six torpedo tubes in the bow.
The overall dimensions of the boat were the same type VII-C/42.
No copy was built and the project was canceled in May 1943.

Typeo VII-D

The type VII-D was a minelayer specialized, designed to launch SMA mines in British coastal waters.
Using the layout of the VII-C, a new section was added aft of the control room.
Five pitchers vertical mine, each consisting of three mines SMA were housed in this new section. The tanks were elongated saddle, allowing a greater capacity of diesel.
The type VII-D was unique in his ability.
Because launchers of mines had been housed in a new section, this meant that the existing structure of the boat was unchanged.
Thus the functions of torpedoes and armament of the boat were fully functional, and this allowed the submarine to play a dual role, as a minelayer or as boat attack.
However, because of its greater size and weight, lost in maneuverability, speed, and time of immersion.
A total of 6 U-Boot Type VII-D were commissioned between August 1941 and January 1942, from U-213 to U-218.

- Displacement: 965 tons (surfaced), 1,080 tons (submerged)
- Length: 76.9 meters
- Width: 6.38 meters
- Draft: 5.01 meters
- Gas oil 169.4 tons
- Propulsion: 2 diesel engines F46 6-cylinder 1,400 hp, two electric motors of 375 hp
- Batteries: 124 elements AFA 33 MAL 800 E (9,160 Ampèere)
- Autonomy: 11,200 miles nautical (10 knots surfaced), 5,050 miles nautical (16 knots surfaced), 69 nautical miles (4 knots submerged)
- Torpedo tubes: 4 forward, 1 aft
- Refills: 12
- Mine: 26 TMA or 39 TMB or 15 SMA 350 kg
- 1 88 mm gun C35 L / 45 with 220 strokes

- Two 20 mm cannons Flak C30 (2 x 1) with 4,380 hits
- 1 gun 37mm Flak with 1,195 hits
- Four 20 mm cannons C38 (2 x 2) with 4,380 hits
- Crew: 44 men (4 officers and 40 crew members)

Type VII-E

This was a purely experimental version to test the performance of a new diesel engine V-12 two times.
The weight saving achieved by a lightweight engine would be used for a thicker armor, allowing a greater depth of immersion. The program, however, was closed and the type VII-E never saw the light

Type VII-F

The type VII-F is born with the role of supply torpedoes for other U-boats, in order to avoid the return to port.
A new section is inserted before the control room to contain 24 torpedoes, arranged in four layers.
An additional door with a pulley system to allow these torpedoes to be transferred between the submarines on the high seas.
Although, in theory, it sounded good, in practice the physical transfer of torpedoes at sea rarely worked.
This, in fact, involved two submarines fixed together in the open sea, not able to dive and practically vulnerable to enemy fire until the transfer had been completed.
The work was slow and laborious, and the practice was quickly interrupted.
A total of four U-Boot Type VII-F were commissioned by U-1059 U-1062.

The U-29 was a German submarine type VII-A at the service of the Kriegsmarine. He participated in the Battle of the Atlantic sank 13 ships, including the aircraft carrier British Corageous. Was sunk by its own crew Kupfermühle May 4, 1945.

Finished to complete construction sites AG Weser (Bremen) August 29, 1936, the U-29 entered service with the Kriegsmarine November 16 of the same year under the command of Heinz Fischer, who remained in this position until 31 October 1938, when the next day he was succeeded Georg-Heinz Michel, who in turn gave way to the April 4, 1939 Kapitänleutnant (Lieutenant) Otto Schuhart, with which the U-29 received all his successes. On 19 August 1939 he started in Wilhelmshaven the first of seven war patrols that the U-29 he performed in his career. On September 8, was hit with four guns and then sank the tanker British Regent Tiger, 402 km south-west of the island of Cape Clear (Southern Ireland), on September 13 it was the turn of the tug British Neptunia to which beside the day after the tanker, also British, British Influence, stop with two cannon shots 290 km south-west of Cape Clear, evacuated and then sank. The commander of the U-Boot Otto Schuhart did shoot the flares in the air to attract the attention of rescuers and stopped the Norwegian freighter Ida Bakke, neutral, indicating the position of the British sailors, who were all saved.

The biggest win of the U-29, however, came September 17, 1939 against the British aircraft carrier Courageous by 22,500 tons. Schuhart sighted the big ship (escorted by four destroyers) at 18:00, at 19:50 but only managed to bring in a good position to launch torpedoes, two of which hit the Courageous which sank 17 minutes after about 306 km south-west of the island of Dursey.

The destroyer Ivanhoe attacked with depth charges the U-Boot for four hours, but procured only minor damage and men of Schuhart came out unscathed. The admiralty instead withdrew all aircraft carriers by hunting U-boats. On September 26, 1939, the U-29 ended the cruise in Wilhelmshaven.

No noteworthy events the second patrol, started on 14 November in Wilhelmshaven and finished in the same city December 16, 1939. Was better in the next sortie, which began February 6, 1940, as the British merchantman sank after hitting Cato, on March 3, a naval mine left by U-29 4 km west of Nash Point.

The next day Schuhart and his men sank the British merchant Thurston and Pacific Reliance, the first 52 km west of Trevose Head, the second north of Land's End, then returned to Wilhelmshaven March 12, 1940.

On April 17, the U-29 left for a trip transfer in Trondheim where docked April 23, only to return to patrol war, finished winless or special events, in Wilhelmshaven on May 4th.

May 16 was given to Otto Schuhart the Knight's Cross of the Iron Cross and the 27th of the same month the submarine began its fifth cruise of war. After nearly a month of navigation and replenished after the German ship anchored in Vigo Bessel June 20, the U-29 sighted near Cape Finisterre the merchant greek Dimitris, sunk with cannon 88 mm placed on the deck; in the same way on 1 July was sunk the merchant greek Adamastos south-west Ireland. The last two successes of the German patrol came in two days later, on 2 and 3 July: at 13:45 of the second U-29 cannon opened fire on the Panamanian freighter Santa Margarita, sunk, and at 2:10 of the July 3 was given the coup de grace with a torpedo the British tanker Athellaird, remained isolated from the convoy to which he belonged.

On 11 July 1940, the German submarine was back in Wilhelmshaven. After over a month of rest at the U-29 was ordered to move on 2 September in Bergen, where September 5 left for the sixth war patrol which yielded the last sinking the German submarine: it was the British merchantman Eurymedon , hit September 25 with two torpedoes 589 km west of Achill Head and sank two days later.

The cruise ended, in fact, in Lorient on 1 October 1940 and the last exit in the sea, which began October 26 and ended on 3 December in Wilhelmshaven, was not sunk any enemy ship.

On January 2, 1941, the U-29 was withdrawn from the front line and relegated to secondary tasks or training until April 17, 1944. Otto Schuhart was replaced as of January 3 six commanders that continued until April 17, 1944. The U-29 was sunk by German sailors May 4, 1945 at Kupfermühle to avoid capture by the Allies.

The total tonnage of ships sunk was of 89,777 tons.

- Displacement: 745 tons
- Length: 64.51 meters
- Height: 9.50 meters
- Draft: 4.37 meters
- Operating depth: 220 meters
- Speed: 8 knots (14.82 km/h)
- Autonomy 94 nautical miles at 4 knots (151.28 km to 7.41 km/h)
- Crew: 42-46 men
- Armament: 11 torpedoes, 22 mines and a 88 mm gun

The U-30 was a German submarine type VII-A at the service of the Kriegsmarine. He participated in the Battle of the Atlantic sank 17 ships and damaging two others. Was sunk by its own crew Kupfermühle May 4, 1945.

The sinking of the first ship in World War II, English Athenia, was indeed caused by U-30, September 3, 1939. The U-30 was also the first submarine to enter the base of Lorient July 7, 1940.

Completed August 4, 1936 in yards AG Weser of Bremen, the U-30 entered service on October 8 of the same year under the command of Kapitänleutnant (Lieutenant) Hans Cohausz, which happened from February 15 to August 17, 1938 Hans Pauckstadt, in turn replaced in November by Kapitänleutnant Fritz-Julius Lemp, with which the submarine collected all his successes. On August 22, 1939, the U-30 departed from Wilhelmshaven on her first cruise during which sank his first three merchant, all British: the Athenia from 13,581 tons September 3 (mistaken for an armed merchant 402 km west of Inishtrahull; first ship of World War II to sink into the sea), the Blairlogie from 4,425 tons on September 11 (322 km west of Ireland) and the Fanad Head by 5,200 tons September 14 (451 km north-west of Malin Head).

This ship was the first stop with a cannon shot but the crew managed to send a request for help via radio, so when the men of Lemp boarded the ship to take prisoners and prepare it for the sinking, came a Blackburn Skua took off from the aircraft carrier Ark Royal and dropped bombs too close to the sea surface, falling into the sea hit by shrapnel that still hurt even three German sailors. The U-30 plunged quickly, leaving in the sea, in addition to the wounded, another man, and ten minutes later came another Skua who mistook the wreckage of the plane crashed just before the tower of the submarine, and you dropped bombs over. When the danger seemed to have ceased, Lemp ordered him to re-emerge to retrieve the wounded but at that moment came another Skua that, like the first, sank for throwing bombs too close to the sea. The submarine then recovered six men (four Germans and two British pilots survivors) and soon after launched a torpedo that sank the Fanad Head, just when they were about to occur six Swordfish that severely damaged the now submerged U-30, also reached by bombs depth from the Bedouin and Punjabi, while the Tartar retrieved the survivors of the freighter. After a stop on 19 September in Reykjavik (in Iceland, still not occupied by the British) to leave a seriously injured person, the U-30 returned to Wilhelmshaven September 27 with no other noteworthy events.

Once repaired the damage December 9, 1939 the U-30 left for the open sea but only two days later had to return to Wilhelmshaven because of a fault in the engine occurred at about 60 km west of the Norwegian town of Egersund.

On 23 December 1939, the Kriegsmarine submarine U-30 sailed from Wilhelmshaven for her third war patrol.

At 4:00 on December 28 was sunk the vessel armed British HMS Barbara Robertson (56 km north-west of the Butt of Lewis, in the northern tip of the island of Lewis) whose crew was rescued by the Swedish merchant Hispania, warned its by U-30.

In the early afternoon, however, about 106 km west of the Butt of Lewis, appeared in the eyes of the commander Lemp a well bigger prey, the battleship HMS Barham was launched a torpedo that killed four men but failed to get lay on the seabed the great ship 31,100 tons, which instead joined Liverpool from where he moved to Birkenhead for six months of repairs performed by Cammell Laird. On 11 January 1940, the British merchantman El Oso sank after hitting a mine left by U-30 on January 16, the Gracia, however, had only damaged by another mine while the day after Cairnross, once touched a mine left always by U-30, was not so fortunate, and disappeared into the sea. Lemp and his men returned to Wilhelmshaven so the same January 17 after having sunk three ships and damaged two others.

The fourth and fifth unsuccessful sortie, both started and finished in Wilhelmshaven and held from 11 to 30 March 1940 the first (to signal the rescue of the crew of a Dornier Do 18 crashed March 29 in the North Sea) and the April 3 to May 4, 1940 the second.

On 8 June 1940, the U-30 began, once again from Wilhelmshaven, his sixth cruise during which sank five merchant. The first, the British Otterpool, sank 209 km west of

Ushant on June 20, followed on 22 June by the Norwegian Randsfjord 113 km south-east of Cobh.

The U-30 emerged after the sinking of the boat, offered a bottle of brandy to the survivors and disappeared quickly at the sight of two destroyers in the distance.

The third victory of the cruise came June 28 against the British Llanarth sunk 354 km south of Ushant and the fourth victim came on 1 July with the British merchantman Beignon, destroyed 483 km west of Ushant. Before returning to Lorient July 7 (making it the first German submarine base to exploit the French captured) the U-30 sank the Egyptian merchant Angele Mabro south-west of Brest.

Most disappointing seventh sea trip, which began on July 13, 1940. It was in fact a single ship sank on July 21, the British merchantman Ellaroy 290 km west of Cape Finisterre.

Back in Lorient July 24, U-30 left for her last cruise on August 5, always with Fritz-Julius Lemp in command. Four days later sank the Swedish merchant Canton (113 km west of Tory Island) and August 16, it was the turn of British Clan Macphee 563 km west of North Uist (Outer Hebrides), last ship ever sunk by U-30. The total tonnage sunk by submarine to share climbed to 123,232 tons. The trip ended in Kiel August 30, and Lemp was awarded the Knight's Cross of the Iron Cross in recognition for his actions.

In September 1940 the command of U-30 passed to Robert Prützmann and then to other until the end of the war, but the submarine never returned at the forefront of being assigned to coastal surveillance, including duties of a training ship.

On 4 May 1945, the crew sank to drop it in Allied hands in the Bay of Kupfermühle, in Schleswig-Holstein.

The U-36 was a German submarine type VII-A at the service of the Kriegsmarine. He played a minor role in the Battle of the Atlantic sank three merchant before being in turn sunk in the North Sea December 4, 1939.
The U-36 began its work December 16, 1936 as a submarine training under the command of Kapitänleutnant (naval lieutenant) Klaus Ewerth. This activity ended on 1 August 1939 when already from 1 February 1939, the command was passed to Korvettenkapitän (Lieutenant Commander) Wilhelm Fröhlich, with which the submarine remained until its sinking.

U-36

On August 31, the U-36 came out of Wilhelmshaven on a cruise test returning to Kiel (city where it was built and completed March 2, 1936) on 6 September. The next day began the first war patrol unit and September 15 was sunk Truro British merchantman of 974 tons 241 km east of the lighthouse at Kinnaird Head (West of Scotland).
On September 17, the British submarine Seahorse launched three torpedoes at the U-36 that had just finished checking a neutral merchant of Denmark, but missed and the German submarine managed to escape.

Eight days later, that is, September 25, the U-36 sank his second ship, the cargo of 1,839 tons Swedish Silesia, 72 km north-west of Egerö. On September 27, Fröhlich and his men captured the merchant, also Swedish, Algeria about 32 km west of Skudenes (Rogaland) and it is believed that the Norwegian merchant Solaas of 1,368 tons is sunk the next day hit a mine left by 'U-36, bringing the total tonnage of ships intercepted Allied to 5,798 tons. The submarine returned to Kiel September 30.
On December 2, 1939, the U-36 sailed for her second and final round of patrol since two days later was sunk south-west of Kristiansand by a torpedo of the British submarine Salmon.
All the crew of 40 men died.

The U-47 was a submarine U-Boot Type VII B, released by the Krupp factories Kiel February 25, 1937, and entered service December 17, 1938.

The U-47 became famous after his second mission of war: October 14, 1939, under the command of Günther Prien, entered the naval base of the Royal Navy in Scapa Flow, managed to sink the British battleship HMS Royal Oak.

The Royal Oak was anchored at Scapa Flow in the Orkney Islands, when it became the first British warship to be sunk during World War II. The losses were high: the crew of 1,234 men of war, 833 died in the sinking or his injuries.

At strategic level, the loss of a battle ship dating back to the First World War did not change the balance, but a psychological and moral effect was considerable. The author of the sinking, the Kapitänleutnant Günther Prien, instantly became a celebrity, and on his return to Germany he became the first official submariner to be decorated with the Knight's Cross of the Iron Cross.

For the British this attack was also a demonstration of the inadequacy of the harbor defenses, which were then quickly reorganized and strengthened. Currently the Royal Oak lies upside down in the same place where it sank; the water is deep at that point about thirty meters, and the keel of the ship is 5 meters below the water surface. The wreck is officially a war grave. Every year, on the anniversary of the sinking, divers of the Royal Navy explain a flag on the stern of the ship. As the war grave is prohibited approach to all other sub.

After this success led eight other combat missions, remaining at sea for 238 days and sank 30 merchant ships (with a total tonnage of 193,808 tons) and damaging eight others.

Party for the tenth war mission February 20, 1941, the U-47 failed to return to base.

For many years it was believed that the U-47 was sunk by the British destroyer HMS Wolverine, west of Ireland; However, analyzing archival sources, it appeared that this destroyer actually attacked another German submarine, the AU.

Lacking an explanation then ascertained about the fate of the U-47 and its 45 crew members, were formulated many hypotheses: underwater mines, mechanical problems or friendly fire, are just some of the possible causes of the sinking of this submarine.

Karl Doenitz, commander of the German submarines, began from the first days of the war to study a plan to attack Scapa Flow. The purpose was twofold: first, a successful attack at Scapa Flow would cause the immediate removal of the ships of the Home Fleet from the area, making it less tight blocking of the Royal Navy in the North Sea and facilitating the attacks Germans to Atlantic convoys; Second, the success of its action striking at Scapa Flow would have symbolic meaning to avenge Hochseeflotte, autoaffondatasi in the same area after the German defeat in World War I.

For this mission Doenitz chose Kapitänleutnant (naval lieutenant) Günther Prien, commander of U-47 and first author of the sinking of the war in the Atlantic, one of the British merchantman Bosnia sunk September 5, 1939, and looked to attack in the night between 13 and 14 October, moonless night and a favorable tide. The preparation of the attack was favored by good quality photos taken in a recent reconnaissance flight, which showed the weakness of the defenses and plenty of possible targets. Doenitz decided then that he would enter Prien at Scapa Flow to the east across the Strait of Kirk, passing north of Lamb Holm, a small island between Burray and Mainland.

Prien initially mistook the passage to the south, called "Strait Skerry", that provided for, but as soon as he realized that the U-47 was heading the wrong step, shallow and blocked by artificial barriers, ordered a quick turn to the northeast.

Surface and illuminated by the dawn boreal, the submarine slipped between the sunken ships Seriano and Numidian, ran aground for a few moments on a cable protruding from Seriano, favorite all the way by the tide and by a strong current. He was also briefly illuminated by the lights of a passing taxi on the shore, but the driver did not give the alarm.

Finally entered the port, at 00:27 on 14 October, Prien wrote the logbook a triumphant "Wir sind in Scapa Flow!" (We are in Scapa Flow!) Before heading south-east for a few kilometers before reversing route. Contrary to the expectations of the

German officer, the area was almost empty; Indeed, Admiral Forbes had ordered to disperse the fleet, doing away so some of the main objectives. The U-47 was directed so far towards four warships at anchor, including Belfast, just come on duty and anchored off the island of Flotta and Hoy, about 8 km away in front of him, in the opposite direction from the channel between the mainland and Lambs Holm from which he had entered, but Prien, not having seen, gave the order to reverse course.

Browsing the opposite direction was sighted the Royal Oak, about 4,000 meters north, correctly identified as a battleship class Revenge. Farther behind him could be seen a second ship, incorrectly identified by Prien as a battleship class Renown and later identified by the German secret service as the Repulse.

In fact it was the old Ark Royal, seaplane of WWI, renamed HMS Pegasus in 1934.

At 0:58 Prien ordered to launch all four torpedo tubes forward, two to the Royal Oak and two to the other goal. Only three were launched, because the fourth torpedo tube had no failure in the launch mechanism. After about three and a half minutes of waiting they heard a single explosion: a torpedo had hit the bow of the Royal Oak, but the explosive charge was detonated altogether because of a malfunction; in the early stages of the conflict malfunctions torpedoes were a very common thing for the Germans. The blast shook the entire unit, however, waking up the crew. Furthermore the anchor starboard was cut cleanly, making much noise. Initially it was suspected an explosion in the storage of flammable materials in the bow, where he had stowed even kerosene. Recalling also the explosion never clarified another warship just to Scapa Flow in 1917, the Vanguard, was ordered over the intercom to control the temperature of the warehouses. Meanwhile, however, many sailors were returned to their bunks, since no one thought to the possibility that the ship was under attack. Meanwhile Prien had given orders to turn to launch a torpedo from the stern, but did not reach the target. Then reloaded tubes bow, gave the order to focus again on the Royal Oak, which was made the target of all three torpedoes launched from about 1,500 meters at 1:14. After about two minutes, to 1:16, all three torpedoes hit in rapid succession the Royal Oak amidships. The shots went to sign were followed by a series of explosions that shook the hull as the ship quickly began to take on water. In a few moments the ship is tilted by about 15° to starboard and consequently the portholes of this side went down below the water level, which began to flood the premises.

A few minutes later the hull tilted further up to 45°, remaining in that position for several minutes before disappearing beneath the surface to 1:29 Thirteen minutes after the second salvo of torpedoes U-47. The dead were 833, including Rear Admiral Henry Blagrove, commander of the 2nd Division battleships.

The tender Daisy 2, conducted by John Gatt of the Royal Naval Reserve had been anchored for the night at the left side of the Royal Oak. After being hit by the second salvo of torpedoes the battleship began tilting to starboard dragging the tender. Gatt ordered to cut the rope that tied the Daisy 2 at the Royal Oak, whose protections antisubmarine were beginning to emerge from the water, raising the small boat until the moorings were removed and the ship was freed in water.

Many of the sailors of the battleship that is launched from Royal Oak during the sinking were dressed in little more than their sleepwear, and were unprepared for the cold waters of October. Also a thick layer of fuel oil had already covered the surface of the water, making it difficult to swim and intoxicating men.

Among those who tried to overcome by swimming the distance of about 800 meters that separated them from the nearest shore, only a few survived.

Gatt, the lights on the tender and was able to save 386 men, including the commander of the Royal Oak, Captain William Benn, in command of the ship from July 7, 1939.

Attempts to rescue lasted for about two and a half hours, until almost 4 am, when Gatt moved away from the area to transport the survivors already embarked on Daisy 2 on Pegasus. Helped by boats of Pegasus and the harbor, was responsible for almost all of the bailouts unsuccessful, act for which he was awarded the Distinguished Service Cross January 1 following, the only decoration awarded in the story of the sinking of the Royal Oak.

The British were initially confused as to the causes of the sinking, suspecting even of a possible explosion on board or in an air strike. Just was found that an attack submarine was the most likely cause were blocked exits from Scapa Flow, but in the meantime, the U-47 had already managed to get away undisturbed.

The BBC gave the news of the sinking in the late morning of 14 October, and the transmission was received by both listening services by the same German U-47. Divers sent to check the hull on the morning of 14 came across the remains of a German torpedo, thus confirming the nature of the attack.

On October 17, the First Lord of the Admiralty Winston Churchill officially announced the loss of Royal Oak in the Commons, admitting that the raid had been "a remarkable success of professional skills and daring", but later declared that the loss had not changed in any way the strategic situation of the war. The German Ministry of Propaganda quickly exploited this success, the minutes of which was broadcast by the popular radio journalist Hans Fritzsche and showed the widespread jubilation in the country. Prien and his crew reached Wilhelmshaven at 11:44 on 17 October, and was immediately hailed as heroes. They learned also that Prien had been decorated with the Iron Cross first class, while all the crew with the Iron Cross second class. Hitler sent his own plane at the base to carry the crew to Berlin, where he decorated personally Prien with the Knight's Cross of the Iron Cross.

This decoration, awarded for the first time in an official submariner, later became the decoration longer used to reward the success of the U-boat commanders.

Prien was nicknamed "the Bull of Scapa Flow" and his crew decorated the tower of the U-47 with an image of a bull snorting, who later became the emblem of the 7th fleet U-Boot.

Prien found himself inundated with requests for investments in radio programs and interviews from the press. The following year was published his autobiography, entitled Mein Weg nach Scapa Flow. In the following years of rumors circulated claiming that Prien had been driven into Scapa Flow by a certain Alfred Wehring, German secret agent who lived in Orkney posing as a Swiss watchmaker named Albert Oertel.

Following the attack would have fled aboard the submarine B-06 back in Germany. This version of events was revealed by an article by journalist Curt Riess of May 16, 1942 in the Saturday Evening Post and was later taken up by other authors and other newspapers. Research conducted after the war in the German archives and Orkney have found no proof nor the existence of such a Oertel, nor a spy named Wehring, nor a submarine called B-06, thus leading to the conclusion that the story was absolutely untruthful.

- Displacement: 753 tons surfaced, 857 tons submerged
- Length: 66.50 meters
- Propulsion: 2 diesel engines from 1400 horses, two electric motors of 375 horsepower
- Speed: 17.9 knots surfaced, 8 knots submerged
- Autonomy: 6.500 nautical miles
- Crew: 45 men
- Armament: one 88 mm gun, one 20 mm anti-aircraft system, 5 torpedo tubes 533 mm (14 torpedoes)

U-69

The U-69 was the first submarine type VII-C to serve in the Kriegsmarine during World War II. This meant that, compared to previous U-Boot, could travel longer, armed with eleven torpedoes, a 88 mm cannon deck for smaller targets and anti-aircraft machine gun to defend against attacks from the sky.

The U-69 sank over 69,000 tons of Allied shipping during a career that lasted two years, making himself one of the U-boats in continuous service who survived longer.

The U-69 was built in the shipyards Germaniawerft of Kiel in 1940, and was completed in November of the same year.

After the maiden voyage in the Baltic Sea (which served to train the crew to the new medium and to repair minor defects), the U-69 was sent into the Atlantic Ocean in February 1941, immediately obtaining success.

The U-69 sank three merchant during his first patrol: February 17, 1941 torpedoed the MV Siamese Prince while 19 came the SS Empire Blanda. Both actions took place in waters around the Faroe Islands, causing total death of 87 sailors, all those on board the two vessels. Five days later, on 24 February, the U-69 sank the SS Temple Moat, who went down with all 42 crewmen.

The second patrol U-69 took place off the coast of West Africa, during which the U-boat was able to lay 16 mines off Lagos and Sekondi-Takoradi, causing the sinking of a British steam and taking advantage of the absence by the Allies in organizing a system of convoys also in African seas.

In total, during his second patrol the U-69 sank nine ships, including the SS Robin Moor, US flag and intercepted off the British port of Freetown in Sierra Leone. The ship was given half an hour to evacuate crew and passengers, who departed aboard lifeboats. After that, the U-69 the pelted with torpedoes and gunfire until it sank. The survivors were left adrift in lifeboats, for eighteen days. The sinking of the Robin Moor provoked a strong reaction in the United States, the nation at that time neutral: President Roosevelt called Germany "an international outlaw" and ordered the closure of all German and Italian consulates on US soil except embassy. Also, after this episode a few shipping companies US continued to feel safe. Time magazine wrote about in June 1941: "If these sinkings continue, US ships directed in areas away from the front of the war will be in danger. So the United States would be forced to draw their boats from the ocean or to enforce their right to freedom of navigation". In October 1941, during the trial for espionage case called "Duquesne Spy Ring", the federal government accused Leo Waalen had radioed in Germany the date of departure of the SS Robin Moor, five days before the last and fatal voyage of the ship. Waalen was found guilty and sentenced to twelve years in prison for espionage and another two years for violation of the Foreign Agents Registration Act, a law enacted in 1938 which called for the self-identification of foreign agents as such.

It took almost a year before the U-69 was able to add another symbol on its turret, that before he could sink another ship. This was caused both by the fact that during the second half of 1941 allies increased the safety of trains and is from a period of bad luck of the same U-69, which for various reasons was forced to return to the base very soon, due to failures mechanical or of diseases among the crew. Indeed, during the fourth patrol, the submarine returned to the base of Saint Nazaire prematurely because the commander Metzler was suffering from renal colic.

It was only in May 1942, after five fruitless patrols, the U-69 added the longed symbol, when bombarded and sank the small vessel James E. Newson off the United States. That seemed to end the bad luck of the submarine, which managed to destroy three more ships the same month, taking advantage of the operation Paukenschlag.

In June 1942, the commander Ulrich Gräf reported to have sunk a large ship near the coast of Suriname, during the passage of the U-69 in the Caribbean Sea. However, after the war it was not possible to identify the alleged boat, and we tend to attribute this discrepancy to an error by the master Gräf.

At 3:25 am on October 14, 1942, the U-96 commander Gräf sank the ferry SS Caribou civil, in the Strait of Cabot. The submarine was for some time in that area, and only the day before had destroyed the SS Carolus, killing eleven sailors.

The Caribou was sighted in the early morning despite having turned off all the lights, mainly because it produced a lot of smoke that loomed, phosphorescent, against the sky. Gräf, taking advantage of the absence of military ships of Commons, he was placed carefully before launching a torpedo.

The Caribou had sailed a few hours before from North Sydney, Nova Scotia, and was directed to Port aux Basques, on the island of Newfoundland, the port where it was usually moored.

The local military authorities had insisted that the ferry extinguished its lights, to make it harder by the sighting of a possible enemy; However, if the lights had been turned on, most likely the U-96 would have recognized as a civilian ship and would not attack. The controversy, which raged in Canada in the following weeks was even more complicated by the fact that on the Caribou there were at least 57 British soldiers, Canadian and US, the fact that virtually legitimized as a military target in all respects. In addition, we also focused on the work of HMCS Grandmere, a minesweeper that accompanied the Caribou (somehow enhancing the appearance of the same military).

Immediately after the explosion, the Grandmere, under the command of Lieutenant Cuthbert, not chased the submarine nor dropped depth charges, preferring instead to immediately start relief operations of the castaways. Lieutenant Cuthbert was criticized both because it risked being attacked in turn, is because the U-69 allowed to leave undisturbed by hiding under the wreckage of the Caribou.

However, the officer refused to apologize, citing the fact that 102 people had been saved thanks to his action. The survivors were taken to Sydney while ships from the island of Newfoundland were collecting corpses floating.

In all, the count of victims recovered from the cold waters of the Atlantic, which at that time only measured 12° C temperature, amounted to 137 deaths: 57 soldiers, 31 members of the merchant marine and 49 civilians, including many women.

The Caribou was the last ship sunk by U-69, and after a fruitless patrol during the winter he met his end in February 1943.

On February 17, 1943, while operating in the "wolf pack" Haudegen, the U-69 was involved in an attack on the convoy ONS 165 in the middle of the North Atlantic. Identified with radar HF/DF, the U-69 was bombarded with depth charges, severely damaged and forced to emerge.

At this point, the destroyer HMS Fame rammed him, destroying leaving no survivors.

The U-69, which is unusual, had two emblems. The first, implemented at the time of entering the service, he was chosen by the first commander, Jost Metzler and consisted of the word Horrido and three pairs of signal flags indicating the letters LMA, a reference to Götz von Berlichingen.

Following the sinking of the HMS Royal Oak by U-47 Günther Prien, was ordered that all the submarines of the 7th fleet, which also belonged to the U-69, U-47 adopt the bull as its emblem. However, it was not included in the orders no illustration, and the first officer of the U-69, Oberleutnant zur See Hans-Jürgen Auffermann, who had never before seen the emblem in question, he saw an image of a French cheese box depicting a cow laughing and decided to paint one on the turret of the U-69, complete the slogan "la vache qui rit" (the cow that laughs).

Metzler when it came to knowledge, he decided to keep it because it made her laugh all who saw her. The crew of the U-69 went so far as to adopt the slogan as their war cry, and the submarine itself was nicknamed the Laughing Cow thereafter.

"The Laughing Cow" was also chosen by Jost Metzler as the title of his memoirs of his time as commander of the U-69, during which he was awarded the Knight's Cross of the Iron Cross. The book was published in 1954.

The U-69 sank sixteen merchant for a total of 69,131 tons of shipping sunk.

The U-81 was a German submarine type VII-C at the service of the Kriegsmarine. He participated in the Battle of the Atlantic and the Mediterranean to the battle and sank a total of twenty-seven ships, including the British aircraft carrier HMS Ark Royal. Was sunk January 9, 1944 in Pula by US bombers.

The U-81 was launched at the Bremer Vulkan-Vegesacker Werft in Bremen-Vegesack February 22, 1941 and entered service with the Kriegsmarine, the German navy, on 26 April, put in command dall'Oberleutnant zur See (Lieutenant of vessel) Friedrich Guggenberger, sponsored Kapitänleutnant (Lieutenant) on 1 September. The U-81 performed its first patrol in the sea under the 1.Unterseebootsflottille (1st Flotilla U-Boot) from July 17 to August 7, 1941, as yet unidentified submarine undergoing development and training. Obtained the status of U-Boot to the forefront on 1 August, the submarine began the 27th of the month from Trondheim, Norway, her second patrol with destination Brest (France), where he arrived September 19th after having sunk two merchant ships to the British off Cape Farewell (9 and 10 September).

Now in order to head to the theater of the Mediterranean, the Kapitänleutnant Guggenberger sailed from Brest with the crew October 29, but the day after he was attacked with depth charges from a Catalina and a Lockheed Hudson British who brought him such damage to force him to return to Brest for the necessary repairs. On November 4, the submarine was able to proceed to sea (initially it was discovered that on board there were charts on the area of operations and the crew had to return to port, losing a few hours of time) by navigating to the Italian port of La Spezia, scoring an instant success for the Axis forces torpedoing November 13 the British aircraft carrier HMS Ark Royal, which sank the next day when towing in Gibraltar.

The destroyer escort threw some bombs deep, but the U-81 was able to get to La Spezia December 10 unscathed. Meanwhile, on 1 December, was passed in the organic 29.Unterseebootsflottille. After a fruitless patrol in the Mediterranean lasted thirty-seven days, the U-81 returned to sink several ships during her fifth patrol, away from La Spezia to the Greek island of Salamis: 16 to 22 April 1942 sank torpedoing, shooting the cannon or ramming, seven ships (one French, one British and five Egyptian small tonnage), also some shelling targets in the port of Haifa (Israel) April 17, in whose waters had also released of naval mines in the two previous days.

Arrived April 25 at Salamis, departed from here on 6 May for another patrol, the sixth, which ended June 3 without noteworthy events. The U-81 was then reassigned to La Spezia and, during the transfer, he was able to sink a British tanker, June 10 off the coast of Alexandria, Egypt, to which were added two other British merchant on 10 and 13 November .

The commander Guggenberger led for the last time the U-81 during the ninth patrol of the submarine, started in La Spezia November 24 and ended on December 21 Pola without any success. December 25, 1942, in fact, the command of the U-81 passed all'Oberleutnant zur See Johann-Otto Krieg, which immediately increased the number of victories of the submarine sinking four ships during a trip from Pula to Salamis.

In subsequent patrols (eleventh, twelfth and thirteenth), shuttling from Salamis in Pula, the U-81 sank a total of eight ships making another useless, running only the danger, June 27, 1943, to be shelled from coastal batteries of Laodicea (Syria), without being damaged. After two more dishes patrols started and finished in Pula, the boat of the Kriegsmarine he signed another success, the last, on November 18, against the British merchantman Empire Dunstan. In the next and last patrol (the seventeenth, from December 30, 1943 to January 3, 1944), in fact, the U-81 is not effected any sinking. On January 9, the following was sunk in the port of Pula in a bombing carried out by US aircraft, during which two crew members also died.

Retrieved April 22, was then dismantled.

The U-96 was a submarine Type VII-C of the German Kriegsmarine, launched September 16, 1939 and entered service September 14, 1940 under the command of Kapitänleutnant Heinrich Lehmann-Willenbrock. Part of the 7th fleet, based in Saint Nazaire (France), the U-96 conducted 11 patrols, sinking 28 ships for a total of 190 094 tons and damaging four more for 33 043 tons. On 30 March 1945, the U-96 was sunk by US bombs in Wilhelmshaven. Throughout the period when it was in service, the U-96 did not suffer losses in the crew. It also became famous for its logo located on the sides of the turret, a sawfish grinning, which became the symbol of the 9th Flotilla when Lehmann-Willenbrock took control in March 1942. During 1941, he boarded the submarine, for a patrol mission, a war correspondent named Lothar-Günther Buchheim. His orders were to photograph and describe a U-boat in action for propaganda purposes. From his experience he wrote a short story entitled "Die Eichenlaubfahrt" and in 1975 a novel which became an international best-seller, entitled "Das Boot" (published in Italy under the title of "U-Boot"), followed in 1976 by the book entitled "U-Boot-krieg", a chronicle of the journey not romanticized. In 1981, Wolfgang Petersen's Das Boot took the novel to the big screen, directing the most expensive German film shot so far, distributed in Italy under the title U-Boot 96, and acclaimed by many as one of the best films of all on submarines times.

- Displacement: 761 tons surfaced, 865 tons submerged
- Length: 67.1 meters
- Width: 6.2 meters
- Propulsion: 2 diesel engines from 1,400 horses, two electric motors of 375 horsepower
- Speed: 17.2 knots surfaced, 7.6 knots submerged
- Autonomy: 6,500 nautical miles at 12 knots surfaced, 80 nautical miles at 4 knots submerged
- Crew: 45 men
- Armament: one 88 mm gun, two 20 mm anti-aircraft systems, five 533 mm torpedo tubes (14 torpedoes).

The U-99 was a submarine U-Boot Type VII-B, particularly famous for being the boat with which Otto Kretschmer, best "ace of U-Boot" of the conflict, he achieved his greatest number of successes. Set March 31, 1939 in yards Germaniawerft of Kiel, was launched March 12, 1940 and entered service April 18, 1940 under the command of Lieutenant Commander Otto Kretschmer. The boat was assigned to 7.Unterseebootsflottille basic first in Kiel and then to Saint Nazaire in occupied France, and embarked on his first patrol operating in June 1940, during which he was slightly damaged by a German plane that had mistaken for an enemy unit. Posted in French base in Lorient, began his first mission in the Atlantic at the end of June 1940, gaining his first success on July 5, 1940, when the boat sank the Canadian freighter Magog off the south coast of Ireland.

In the hands of the expert Kretschmer, U-99 he soon obtained a long series of successes: in the course of eight patrols operating (for a total of 127 days spent at sea), the unit sank 35 merchant ships for a total of 198,218 gross tonnes, and three auxiliary cruisers for a total of 46,440 tons, as well as capture a neutral merchant and damage other five merchant totaling 37,965 tons.

March 16, 1941, the U-99 attacked the convoy HX-112 off the coast of south-eastern Iceland, sinking five merchant, damaging a sixth. The next day, March 17, the boat was detected by the apparatus ASDIC two British destroyers escorting the convoy (HMS Walker and HMS Vanoc), and immediately attacked; severely damaged by depth charges launched HMS Walker, Kretschmer was able to bring out the boat, allowing the commander himself and 40 of the 43 crew members to escape before the final sinking.

The crew was picked up by British ships and taken prisoner.

- Displacement: 753 tons surfaced, 857 tons submerged
- Length: 66.50 m
- Beam: 6.20 meters
- Maximum height: 9.50 meters
- Draught: 4.74 meters

- Propulsion: 2 diesel engines 3,200 hp, two electric motors of 750 hp
- Speed: 17.9 knots surfaced, 8 knots submerged
- Autonomy: 8,700 miles nautical to 10 knots surfaced
- Crew: 45 men
- Armament: one 88 mm gun, one single plant from 20 mm anti-aircraft, five 533 mm torpedo tubes (four bowmen, one aft)

U-100

The U-100 was a German submarine type VII-B in the service of the Kriegsmarine. He participated in the Battle of the Atlantic in command ace Joachim Schepke, sinking 25 ships and damaging other 4. It was sunk by two British destroyers March 17, 1941, in southeast Iceland.

Finished building April 10, 1940 in yards Germaniawerft Kiel, the U-100 entered service May 30 of that year at the controls of Kapitänleutnant Joachim Schepke (Lieutenant), with which the U-Boot attained all its successes.

On August 9, 1940 from Kiel began the first of six war patrols that the U-100 performed throughout its operational life.

The first success came August 16 against the mercantile British Empire Merchant sunk 299 km west of Gweedore. When the U-boats went up to the surface to be sure of victory, observed by the British survivors, Joachim Schepke left the turret but unexpectedly returned to the submarine under water forcing it to quickly close the door out and to cling to the periscope until the Submersible not resurfaced shortly after; the accident was caused by a distraction of staff who was reprimanded by Befehlshaber der U-Boote Karl Doenitz.

The next day, on August 17, the U-boat was spotted by an enemy destroyer which launched 7-8 depth charges but not procured no damage and men of Schepke managed to get away.

On August 25, the British merchantman Jamaica Pioneer stumbled into the network of U-100 which initially missed him with a torpedo, then flipped the cannon of the bridge still without success and finally launched a new torpedo that sank east of Rockall. The apex of the patrol Schepke occurred on August 29 when it sank four merchant (Dalblair, Astra II, Alida Gorthon and Empire Moose, all British except dell'Alida Gorthon) damaging another (the British Hartismere); all ships that are part of the convoy OA-204 sighted at about 209-241 km north-west of Gweedore. The U-100 had completed its first patrol in Lorient on 1 September 1940.

The September 11, 1940 began to Lorient and the second most profitable cruise U-100 with 50,340 tons of shipping sunk. The victories were highly concentrated in the time since starting at 23:10 on 21 September sank the British transport ships Canonesa, Torinia Dalcairn and approximately 547 km west of Bloody Foreland (all part of the convoy HX-72).

The battle continued at 00:22 the next day and have the worst were the merchant Empire Airman, Scholar and Simla (the latter Norwegian) and the tanker Frederick S. Fales.
After seven ships sunk in a short time and with a single torpedo left, the U-100 tried one last attack on Putney Hill, but missed the target and gave up the enterprise, because the merchant was armed and fired three guns . On September 25, the German crew docked in Lorient and Joachim Schepke received the Knight's Cross of the Iron Cross. After the usual days of rest and reorganize the U-100 her lines October 12, 1940 to head back to the west of Scotland. October 18 was damaged the already hit British merchantman Shekatika 145 km south-east of Rockall (then finished by U-123 Karl-Heinz Moehle) and the Dutch merchant Boekelo (also then sunk by U-123). The convoy SC-7, as well as undergo these two attacks, was damaged by U-100 also Blairspey, struck on 19 October. He went worse October 20 to cargo British convoy HX-79 Sitala, Caprella and Loch Lomond, inabissatisi at sea 241 km south-west of Rockall.
On October 21, an oil tanker, failure by torpedoes Schepke, attacked the U-boat with a gun but did no damage; the journey of

the U-100 was still coming towards the end, in fact, on October 23 he returned to Lorient.

The fourth patrol U-100 began November 7, 1940 and yielded seven sunken ships all November 23 and all part of the convoy SC-11, which did not suffer more losses by other U-boats. 0:18 pm to about 258 kilometers west of Bloody Foreland was the first ship to sink the British merchantman Justitia followed about 40 minutes later by the Dutch Ootmarsum, less than twenty minutes after Schepke gave the order to launch a torpedo that sank the Bradfyne. At 04:14 a torpedo broke in half the Norwegian merchant Bruse, twenty minutes later touched at Salonica. The British Leise Mærsk sank 193 km west of Rockall in the first morning, around 8:02, but the U-100 had to wait for the 21:05 to score the last shot of the day against the Dutch merchant Bussum, located 145 km west of Tory Island (Donegal). On November 27, the U-boats returned to Lorient on 1 December Schepke got the Knight's Cross with Oak fronds.

The fifth and penultimate round of the patrol was less bright for the U-100 sank only 17,166 tons of enemy shipping.

Navigation began December 2, 1940 and September 14 were sunk the British merchant Kyleglen and Euphorbia, both southwest of Rockall. The merchant Napier Star sank instead into the evening of 18 December, which was thus to be the last win for Schepke and the U-100.

On 1 January 1941, the U-boats landed in Kiel-where to March 9. After eight days of sailing the U-100 was the first submarine to be spotted and sunk by the use of radar, in this case installed in Vanoc British destroyer that sank with depth charges after it rammed at 03:18 of 17 March 1941, in southeast Iceland, on a cloudy night that would have prevented his identification with the traditional means.

38 German sailors were killed, including the commander Joachim Schepke, while only six men were saved.

The U-Boot 455 type VII-C was whisked away April 2, 1944 while, left the North Africa was heading, as orders received, to the port of La Spezia, considered safer than Toulon. The submarine, remain unknown to this day is the cause of its loss (a drifting mine, an accident on board) is why instead of heading to La Spezia on the German submarine commander decided to continue heading north".

Today the German submarine mysteriously disappeared and reported missing April 6, 1944 we know almost everything: from the ten missions in the Mediterranean to the ship sunk by the name of those who had come and gone at his command to the identity of the 51 men who formed the crew .

The U-Boot 455 did not show up to the appointment and, not having been heard on April 6, was considered lost for unknown cause. And 'This is the mystery that, after identification by now some of the boat, today more than ever fascinated scholars and researchers and, above all, because he was in the area between Portofino and Camogli.

The U-455, commanded by Lieutenant Hans-Martin Scheibe, entered the Mediterranean in the month of January 1944 after ten combat missions carried out in the Atlantic, missions that brought him to sink three merchant ships for 17,685 tons and carry out the laying of two dams mined, the first in the waters of the United States, the second along the Moroccan coast near Casablanca. The submarine belonged to the German Submarine Flotilla VII of Saint Nazaire and arrived in Toulon February 3, from Lorient, only to be officially affiliated to the XXIX Flotilla in the Mediterranean on 2 March.

The 'U-455, sailed from Toulon - the main base of the XXIX Flotilla - February 22 for its tenth and final mission.

The U-Boot 455, however, did not have the opportunity to launch attacks against the numerous Allied shipping transiting in the focal area of traffic, where German submarines of Flotilla XXIX obtained between April and early May, their latest successes, before being swept away by the Mediterranean defensive organization of the Anglo-Americans, made the tactic Swam (search method).

This was the reason why the U-455 and U-230, returning from their missions of war, were diverted exceptionally in La Spezia, which at that time was a more quiet harbor of Toulon and possessed an arsenal at the time perhaps more efficient. Two submarines, the U-230, arrived in La Spezia on 24 February, and then again April 6 to reach Toulon three days later.

If the U-455 was to reach La Spezia - passing, for the shortest route and less guarded by the enemy, ie the tip rounded Cape Corso northern Corsica before crossing, as was logical, the Ligurian Sea with a direct route and in immersion of day to reach the point "C" - what was going to do the submarine much more to the northwest between Portofino and Camogli about 2 miles from the coast?

For more without having received a direct order from his command and entering an area heavily mined by the Germans (the dam "Rettici" that began from the area immediately south and west of the promontory of Portofino to extend towards Genoa almost to Nervi), in a particularly dangerous and not recommended without the support of a ship pilot?

And 'This is the mystery that, after identification by now some of the boat, today more than ever fascinated scholars and researchers. The wreck lies on a muddy bottom of 120 meters, with the end of the bow to 85 meters tilted about 45-50 °, the emerging part of the mud (virtually intact) has a length of about 50 meters. Probably its unusual structure is due to the presence, in the forward area of compartments not flooded; in the vicinity of the wreck are scattered debris on the bottom of the stern disintegrated by the explosion.

The U-558 was a submarine type VII-C of the Kriegsmarine.
Before being destroyed by US and British bombers July 20, 1943, sank 19 ships military and commercial for a total of nearly 100,000 tons. Set January 6, 1940 in the shipyards of Blohm & Voss in Hamburg and launched on 23 December of the same year, the U-558 entered officially entered service in February 20, 1941 under the command dell'Oberleutnant zur See Günther Krech. Based in Brest, on the Atlantic coast of France, the U-558 completed ten patrols during his career at sea. During the first two, which lasted respectively from 1 June to 9 July and from 28 July to 7 August 1941 did not report actions worthy of note and returned each time to port without having had contact with enemy ships. During the third patrol (25 August to 16 September 1941), he came in the British convoy OS 4, about 330 miles north-west of Fastnet Rock, and August 28 torpedoed and sank the cargo ship 10,300 tons Otaio, making 13 casualties among the crew of 71 sailors: the 58 survivors, including the commander Kinnell, were taken to safety by the destroyer HMS Vanoc and landed in Liverpool.

The fourth patrol, which began on October 11, 1941, took off the 15th with the sinking of the lone Canadian merchant from 9,472 tons Vancouver Island, killing all 105 people on board.

Although the U-558 saw the survivors who descended in the lifeboats, when the British corvette HMS Dianthus arrived on the scene to rescue found no castaway still alive. Days later, on 31, a lifeboat with the bodies of two officers of Vancouver Island was found adrift from another vessel of the Royal Navy.

On October 17, the U-558 was part of the "wolf pack" of U-boats that launched a devastating attack on the convoy SC 48, in the North Atlantic. During the battle, the U-558 sank four ships: the corvette escort HMS Gladiolus (925 tons), the British Steam WC Teagle (9,552 tons) and Norwegian merchant Erviken and Rym, respectively 6,595 and 1,369 tons. Later, the submarine was bombed by depth charges from a Catalina flying boat, without causing significant damage. He returned to Brest on 25 October.

The fifth patrol, which began November 24, 1941, was abruptly interrupted when December 2 an aircraft of the Royal Air Force sighted the U-558 that was attempting to cross the Strait of Gibraltar into the Mediterranean Sea.

The aircraft called reinforcements, attracting two English ships that chased the submarine, damaging it severely with the repeated firing of depth charges. Despite this, the U-boats managed to escape and returned to Brest 7 after only fourteen days of sailing and no enemy ship sunk.

Repair work continued until February 10, 1942, when the U-558 was finally able to put to sea for her sixth patrol. Eleven days later, on February 21, with five other U-boats formed a "pack of wolves" who ambushed the convoy ONS 67.

In the clash, eight Allied ships were sent to peak and two others damaged. 24, the U-558 torpedoed the tanker English Anadara, who managed to escape momentarily before being finished, shortly after, by another German submarine, the U-587.

The same day, the U-558 sank the Norwegian tanker Eidanger (9,432 tons) and the steam from English Inverarder 5,578 tons.

On March 11, at last, the submarine returned to Brest.

A month later, on April 12, began his seventh and fruitful patrol off the Atlantic coast of the United States. On May 12, sank off the island of Ocracoke (North Carolina), the HMT Bedfordshire (in peacetime a trawler, then adapted to the requirement and antisubmarine warfare by the Royal Navy at the outbreak of hostilities), sent by Britain to help the US Navy to counter the German U-boats.

Six days later, on 18, fell victim to the U-558 from the Dutch merchant ship 1,254 tons Fauna, which was followed, on 21, the Canadian Boat to 1,925 tons Troisdoc, torpedoed in the Caribbean Sea with no casualties among the crew (which was then carried to safety by a vessel of the US Coast Guard).

23, touched the merchant with stars and stripes by 7,061 tons William Boyce Thompson, who was hit by torpedoes but managed to take refuge in Guantanamo Bay, where he had to be repaired. Months later, on 7 July 1943, William Boyce Thompson met his end at the hands of another U-Boot, this time the U-187. 25, the U-558 attacked the American merchant ship from 3,451 tons Beatrice: the torpedo on the Saint was a failure and did not explode on impact, forcing the submarine to surface and to target the boat with the deck gun.

The arrival of a PBY Catalina seaplane armed with depth charges forced the U-558 to move away, and still have caused enough damage to reduce the ship on fire in a wreck that sank after fifteen hours; the crew of the merchant began to safety on lifeboats, one of which ended up on the firing line of the submarine with the subsequent death of a sailor, the only loss human action. Always in the Caribbean, 27 the U-558 sank the transport from 2,622 tons Jack, belonging to the US Army and at that moment full of sugar. The last sinking of the patrol was to the Dutch merchant ship Triton, by 2,087 tons, which was intercepted 470 miles southeast of Bermuda and sunk by gunfire. The crew of 36 men began to safety on lifeboats, suffering six deaths. After the merchant had now sunk, the U-558 came to the survivors, he received information on the ship that had just sunk and provided help to the shipwrecked, showing them the route to follow to Puerto Rico.

On June 21, 1942, the U-558 completed its seventh patrol returning to Brest after having sunk six ships and damaged one.

On July 29, he left again Brest to begin his eighth patrol.

On August 25, he met the English merchant from 1,987 tons Amakura, who had been part of the convoy WAT 15 but that was left behind, and torpedoed about 90 miles south-east of Port Morant, Jamaica. On September 13, the U-558 sighted the convoy TAG 5, attacked him and sank the cargo ship British Empire Lugard (7,241 tons) and the Dutch Surinam (7,915 tons). The same day, the Norwegian tanker torpedoed also Vilja (6,672 tons), whose crew abandoned it in haste; four hours later, seeing that the ship was sinking, sailors climbed aboard and, finding badly damaged as to be judged, then hopeless, her back to Port of Spain. On the way, they took on board the survivors of the Empire Lugard, another victim of the U-558. The last was the merchant ship sunk US Commercial Trader, from 2,606 tons; spotted 75 miles east of Trinidad, September 16 was torpedoed and sank. On October 16, the U-558 returned to port having sunk, during its eighth patrol, four ships and damaged a fifth.

The submarine remained in port for the rest of 1942, taking up the sea January 9, 1943, for his ninth patrol, during which sank only one ship, the tanker British Empire by 9,811 tons Norseman. The Empire Norseman had been part of the convoy UC 1, was hit and damaged by U-boat U-382 and U-202 to the point of inducing the crew to abandon it, leaving it adrift, reduced to a wreck in which the U-558 had only deliver the coup de grace. On March 23, the submarine returned to Brest.

The tenth and final patrol began on May 8, 1943, and was soon marred by many difficulties: having sighted a convoy, the U-558 tried to position themselves for the attack but was forced to flee from a destroyer; July 14, a Wellington No.224 Squadron RAF attacked him in vain with depth, in exchange for being damaged by anti-aircraft fire U-Boot; three days later, on 17, a Liberator squadron No.224 on the U-558 dropped 24 depth charges from 35 pounds and the boat was saved plunging rapidly while managing to damage the bomber, already in trouble because of malfunctioning bombs, with their anti-aircraft weapons.

On July 20, the U-558 was sighted in the Bay of Biscay by another Liberator, this time the 19th Bomber Squadron US Air Force, who pelted them with the submarine depth charges. However, the U-boat commander Krech returned fire and shot down the aircraft.

The same day, a second Liberator of the 19th Squadron returned to attack the U-558: this time, the bombing caused extensive damage to the submarine, making him unable to dive. The German anti-aircraft fire of the boat forced the American plane to retreat, giving way to a Halifax bomber No.58 Squadron RAF. The damage done to the submarine were serious, seawater infiltrated the battery compartment electrical, toxic chlorine developed by the following chemical reaction and killed many German sailors. The survivors, most of them poisoned by the gas, tried to leave the rundown U-Boot on the boat's edge.

The Halifax English strafed several times shipwrecked, leaving forty bodies to float in an area of a quarter mile around the wreck. A Handley Page Halifax, the model to which belonged the bomber who ended the U-558.

At the end of the action, eight men original crew of 52 sailors were still alive on the boat: one died from drinking seawater, two other unknown causes, leaving only five survivors including the commander Krech, wounded back and thigh.

A US plane arranged to drop a tank of drinking water for them, allowing them to survive until they were finally rescued and taken prisoner by the Canadian destroyer HMCS Athabaskan.

The survivors, after being medicated and fed, were questioned by the Naval Intelligence Division of the Royal Navy, which could not be gouged them anything interesting: as it was written in the final report, "the prisoners are either comparatively ignorant or trained not to speak , and could only be obtained little information of value. " In particular, in the same document describes Krech as a commander "cold, efficient and serious, very respected by his men".

The prisoners were interned as prisoners of war, and were able to return to their homes after the war ended. The only commander of U-558, Günther Krech, who during the war had been decorated with the Iron Cross for sinking 130,000 tons of enemy shipping, would have died June 3, 2000 in Wuppertal.

The construction of the U-977 was assigned to the Blohm & Voss in Hamburg on July 24, 1942 and the submarine was launched March 31, 1943.
On May 6 of that year he was placed under the command of Kaptleutnant zur See (Lieutenant) Hans Leilich for the usual period of exercise in the Baltic. But a series of accidents during maneuvers in which it had to be proven on-board instrumentation created such serious damage to the estate of the hull that the high command of the Kriegsmarine they ordered the use only as a school boat. In mid-December 1944 the lieutenant Heinz Schaeffer took command of the unit, which continued until the end of January 1945 to make travel exercise for crews in training. Then came the sudden transfer order to Hamburg to do the repairs. Released from the dry docks of the port of Hamburg March 31, the U-977 sailed in the direction of Kiel, where the first to April 12 loaded food and ammunition.
It is at this point that Schaeffer was ordered to lead his unit to Norway to be framed in the XXXI flotilla U-Boot.
The trip transfer proves rather difficult.
After a brief stop in Frederikshavn in Denmark, in the subsequent crossing of the Skagerak German submarine must immerse four times because of air raid warnings and stays for six hours underwater in the Oslo Fjord.
On April 30, the U-977 finally enters the port of Kristiansand (Norway). Days are excited; the German Navy, as the other forces of the Reich, is in disarray.
Hitler has just committed suicide in the bunker in Berlin. The news comes via radio also in Norwegian bases of German U-boats. However, the war is not yet over and that Schaeffer receives orders are to set sail as soon as possible; The mission: to reach the trade routes of the Allied convoys leaving the English port of Southampton. After refueling sunny 85 tons of fuel, the fuel becomes scarce in port.
At 22.00 hours in Berlin on May 2, 1945, with the cover of darkness, the U-977 leaves the base of Kristiansand. So begins the adventure of U-977.

Its captain and the crew did not know yet that that last mission will be transformed into a journey that will make history in the maritime environment as an amazing feat. In fact the first days of sailing are relatively quiet.

The submarine proceeds along the Norwegian coast in diving to avoid aerial reconnaissance English, using the Snorkel for 3/4 hours each night to recharge the batteries of electric motors.

The unconditional surrender of the German armed forces signed on May 8, takes the U-977 still sailing along the Norwegian coast. Orders branched via radio to unit commanders in the mission include the immediate cessation of all belligerent action and the obligation to sail immediately to the port closest ally, where surrender and hand over to the port authorities enemy boat intact. Schaeffer and other sized, however, in those moments excited can not know if the message has been manipulated whole or in part before being transmitted.

The commander calls so all the crew, which offers the choice between two solutions: the yield in an English port or groped to reach the Atlantic and then to route to Argentina, the country pro-German, where to deliver the U- Boot. According to calculations by the officer's car, which in the end will prove to be accurate, naphtha is enough to make the trip, but by saving the maximum consumption commander is convinced that with a little 'luck you can evade the British and earn the ocean.

Most people vote for the latter.

On May 10, the U-977 approaching at night Norwegian island of Holsenoy to allow twelve men, all married, who had voted against the hypothesis of the long and dangerous journey, reaching aboard three lifeboats the land and find some way to be reunited with their families in Germany (they were all captured by British troops stationed in Norway).

The U-977, with its crew consists of the remaining thirty-two men between officers, non-commissioned officers and sailors, glides silently through the channel of Iceland in the north of England towards the end of May. To optimize the naphtha and to become invisible to the enemy Schaeffer ago navigate the submarine day at a depth of 50 meters with the electric motors, while at night it comes into operation the two diesel powered by Snorkel, a long tube that during the immersion phase serves to convey the fresh air of the surface in the engine room to operate the motors.

During continuous scuba diving, stale air and the humid heat that are found in the other rooms of the submarine support growth of a thick layer of mold and rust on all interior surfaces (the commander of U-977 in notes his diary which also supplies food not canned were now turned green with mold and the men had all the symptoms of vitamin deficiency).

The breath of the crew due to low oxygen is increasingly difficult. Waste must be expelled out through one of the rooms of launching torpedoes. Schaeffer, among other things, decides not to deprive yourself of torpedoes even if, in doing so, he would earn space and above all lightness, which would have resulted in lower fuel consumption for propulsion.

This decision will be useful to the commander of the U-977 when, once arrived in Argentina, will demonstrate to American authorities who will question him about not attacking any enemy ship after the cease-fire as he tried the equipment intact torpedoes the submarine.

In mid-Atlantic only once the U-977 goes to share periscope when it is to cross the route of a luxury liner. For an hour the submarine holds the wake of the ship then decided to return to the desired course for lack of fuel. This was the luck of unsuspecting passengers of that ship.

The problem of the consumption of fuel oil, in effect, begins to haunt increasingly the commander of U-977.

Traveled 1800 miles marine almost half of the fuel has been consumed; to come in sight of the coasts of South America there are still 5500 miles. The nervousness meanders between the crew Schaeffer but not panicked and ordered to reduce to ten hours sailing with diesel engines and to decrease the speed of a node. If necessary, if that was not enough, as the commander had the extreme decision to route to the nearest Brazil instead of trying to reach the shores of Argentina. Schaeffer understands that the enforced idleness of a large part of the crew fomenting quarrels between men and feeds their pessimism (the worst incident was the second in command of the mutiny, which damages voluntarily periscope) and orders a meticulous maintenance apparatuses U-Boot; each bolt should be checked and tightened. On July 14, the German submarine comes into view of the archipelago of Cape Verde. After more than two months of scuba diving is ordered surfacing near a desert island. The U-977 remains at anchor for four hours. The crew can finally go out on deck, walk on the deck and dive into the crystal clear waters of the island.

Thanks to the hand grenades and harpoons is also caught fresh fish. An attempt to land on the nearby island with a lifeboat fails because of the waves. On board there is a great deal to do with sheet metal and other material of luck tower of the submarine is disguised as a funnel. The intent of the commander is to continue browsing the surface deceiving from afar any ships that the U-Boot will cross posing as a small merchant ship. The day after the trip resumes. On July 23, the U-977 passes the Equator but while on board we celebrate the event with a ritual called "the ceremony of Neptune", as in the tradition of the German submariners, you hear the sound of a plane in the distance. Schaeffer order "battle stations."

Fortunately, the Germans the low profile of a U-boat in the ocean is not so easy to scorgersi. Approaching the coast of Argentina is presented, however, another problem to be solved: the lack of detailed maps of the ports of the coastal cities.

Besides the submarine would have to operate in the North Atlantic and then was equipped with cards for that sector.

You try to mitigate this lack realizing sudden map with the help of geographical indications of a small encyclopedia on board. On July 30, the ship's radio picks up an American radio station announcing the transfer of the US commander of the German submarine U-530 Otto Wermuth and his men, after July 10 had surrendered Argentine entering the port of Mar del Plata.

The news creates panic among the men of U-977, all those miles and then be delivered equally as prisoners.

Many aim to bring the coast, sinking the submarine and smuggled into Argentina.

Schaeffer fails yet again to reason with men. The U-Boot does not absolutely had scuttled, had to surrender in the hands of the Argentine authorities, however, at the risk of being later extradited to the USA as had happened to the crew of U-530.

Indeed, the episode of Boot dell'U- Wermuth convinces the commander of U-977 to choose as a landing Mar del Plata.

The captain and crew of the U-977, after the surrender of the Argentine authorities in Mar del Plata, were extradited to the USA. Schaeffer spent several months in a prison camp for officers, near Washington, during which he had to respond, during several interrogations, accusations of having torpedoed the Bahia, a Brazilian steamer (the ship was sunk July 4th 1945 when he was in the Atlantic Ocean midway between the Brazilian and African coasts due to a mysterious explosion), but the torpedoes supplied U-977 were all still on board at the time of surrender. Moved to London, was placed under investigation again this time on charges that he illegally landed illustrious figures of the Nazi regime in Argentina before surrendering.

Schaeffer was released in 1947.

After several failed attempts to find work in Germany he returned to Argentina, where he built a new life. In the fifties Schaeffer published a book containing his memoirs with which he tried once again to clarify the only real reasons that long journey and permanently remove from himself the suspicion of being one of the last servants of the Hitler regime.

The U-977 was transferred to the US to study its technology.

It was sunk in 1946 by the US submarine Atule during exercise launch torpedoes in which he made from floating target.

The U-977 was in force at the VU-Boot Flottille, from 6 May 1943 to 30 September 1943; the XXI U-Boot Flottille from 1 October 1943 to 28 February 1945; XXXI to the U-Boot Flottille from May 1 to May 8, 1945.

Since May 6, 1943 until February 28, 1945, the U-977 was commanded by Hans Kaptleutnant Leilich.

Since March 1, 1943 August 17, 1945 al dall'Oberleutnant HeinzSchaeffer.

U-995

The U-995 belonged to the VII-C variant of which 577 copies were built well.

It was 67 meters long, 6.2 wide and had a draft of 4.8 meters.

Its operational depth reached 120 meters and the maximum is 300 meters. Displacement of 760 tons surfaced and 865 underwater. Equipped with two diesel engines and two electric reached a top speed of 17 knots on the surface and 7.6 knots submerged. He was armed with 14 torpedoes, two twin machine guns and a heavy machine gun.

It had a crew of 44 men.

Operating in the Arctic seas, sank five ships for a total of 9,062 tons. After the war he was assigned to Norway, but returned later to Germany and placed it on the beach in Laboe, Baltic Sea, building into a museum.

Type IX

Derived from the previous prototype Type IA, the U-Boot Type IX was designed as a U-Boot outreach with much more autonomy on how much could be achieved by the type VII.
The U-Boot Type IX worked so far to reach the Caribbean, the South Atlantic and also the Indian Ocean. The submarine type IX were naturally more wide variations Type VII, to be able to carry enough fuel and equipped to operate in the long periods of patrolling, but was handicapped with a dipping time was slow and more vulnerable to attack thanks to its large size .

U-505, a U-Boot Typ of IX, on display in Chicago

This made them unsuitable for some of the theaters of operations such as in particular the Mediterranean Sea, where the large size were considered a disadvantage in the light of the Allied aerial presence. Used a 9-cylinder turbocharged diesel engine instead of the standard 8-cylinder type VII.
To balance the weight in May, the engine room was situated immediately behind the control room. The Type IX had a double hull filled with the outer hull that surrounded almost completely

the hull under pressure; the upper deck, wide and flat, provided the additional space to house ten torpedoes externally in watertight containers. He had four torpedo tubes forward and two behind, with a total capacity of 22 torpedoes.

More than 200 U-Boot Type IX were built in seven sub-classes.

Type IX-A

The original variant of type IX, launched for the first time in 1938 and built in 8 specimens (from U-37 to U-44) equipped with three telescopes, two in the turret and one in the control room.

- Displacement: 1,032 tons (surfaced), 1,153 tons (submerged)
- Length: 75.5 meters
- Width: 6.5 meters
- Draft: 4.7 meters
- Gas Oil: 154 tons
- Maximum speed: 18.2 knots (surfaced), 7.7 knots (submerged)
- Propulsion: 2 diesel engines 9-cylinder MAN M9V40/46 from 4,400 hp, two electric motors SSW OJ 345/34 from 740 kW
- Autonomy: 10,500 nautical miles (at 10 knots surfaced), 8,100 miles nautical (12 knots surfaced), 65 nautical miles (4 knots submerged)
- Depth: 150 meters (operational), 225 meters (maximum)
- Immersion time: 35 seconds
- Torpedo tubes: 4 forward and 2 aft
- Refills: 8 internal, external 7
- Cannons: 1 naval cannon 10.5 cm SK C/32 to 105 mm, 3 antiaircraft 2 cm FlaK 20 mm, 1 antiaircraft 3.7 cm FlaK M42U 37 mm
- Crew: 4 officers and 44 crew members

Type IX-B

This first improvement to the Type IX summarizes the history of evolution of this class: mainly the search for a range as wide as possible: the fuel is increased from 154 tons to 165 tons, with a range extended to 8,700 nautical miles , however, sacrificing the speed performance.
Apart from that, this model, launched for the first time in 1938, is similar in most features to Type IX-A.

14 units built so designated:
- from U-64 to U-65
- from U-103 to U-111
- from U-122 to U-124

- Displacement: 1,051 tons (surfaced), 1,178 tons (submerged)
- Length: 76.5 meters
- Width: 6.8 meters
- Draft: 4.7 meters
- Gas Oil: 123 tons
- Maximum speed: 18.2 knots (surfaced), 7.3 knots (submerged)
- Propulsion: 2 diesel engines 9-cylinder MAN M9V40/46 from 4.400cv, two electric motors SSW GU345/34 from 740 kW
- Autonomy: 12,000 nautical miles (at 10 knots surfaced) 8,700 miles nautical (12 knots surfaced), 64 nautical miles (4 knots submerged)
- Depth: 150 meters (operational), 225 meters (maximum)
- Immersion time: 35 seconds
- Torpedo tubes: 4 forward and 2 aft
- Refills: 22
- Cannons: 1 105mm naval gun, three anti-aircraft 20 mm, 1 37 mm naval gun
- Crew: 48 men (4 officers and 44 crew members).

Type IX-C

This second variant of the Type IX extended the autonomy of this series until 11.000 nautical miles, which was a significant improvement over its predecessors. Launched for the first time in 1939, the project remained relatively stable for a total of 54 units produced in total thus designated:

- from U-66 to U-68
- from U-125 to U-131
- from U-153 to U-160
- from U-161 to U-166
- from U-171 to U-176
- from U-501 to U-524

Improvements to the propulsion system also helped to maintain performance on a par with the previous type IX.

- Displacement: 1,120 tons (surfaced), 1,232 tons (submerged)
- Length: 76.8 meters
- Width: 6.8 meters
- Draft: 4.7 meters
- Maximum speed: 18.3 knots (surfaced), 7.3 knots (submerged), 6 knots (mode Schnorchel)
- Propulsion: 2 diesel engines 9-cylinder MAN M9V40/46 to 4,400cv, two electric motors SSW GU345/34 from 740 kW
- Gas Oil: 208 tons
- Autonomy: 13,450 nautical miles (at 10 knots surfaced) 11,000 miles nautical (12 knots surfaced) 63 nautical miles (4 knots submerged)
- Depth: 150 meters (operational), 225 meters (maximum)
- Immersion time: 37 seconds
- Torpedo tubes: 4 forward and 2 aft
- Refills: 22
- Cannons: 1 105mm naval gun, 1 gun Flak 37 mm, 1 gun Flak 20
- Crew: 48 men (4 officers and 44 crew members).

Type IX-C/40

This was the most numerous variant of the Type IX series, with 87 units completed during 1944 so designated:
• from U-167 to U-170
• from U-183 to U-194
• from U-525 to U-550
• from U-801 to U-806
• from U-841 to U-846
• from U-853 to U-858
• from U-865 to U-870
• from U-877 to U-882
• from U-889 to U-891
• from U-1221 to U-1235

Even if they had been ordered more, many were canceled to prepare the production of Type XXI. Launched for the first time in 1941, this variant allowed a reach even higher than that of its predecessors, although it was similar to them for all other characteristics.

- Displacement: 1,144 tons (surfaced), 1,257 tons (submerged)
- Length: 76.8 meters
- Width: 6.9 meters
- Draft: 4.7 meters
- Maximum speed: 18 knots (surfaced), 7 knots (submerged)
- Propulsion: 2 diesel engines 9-cylinder MAN M9V40/46 to 4,400cv, two electric motors SSW GU345/34 from 740 kW
- Batteries: 124 items 36 MAK 740 (5,650 amperes) or 124 elements 44 MAL 740 (11,300 amperes)
- Autonomy: 13,850 miles nautical (10 knots surfaced) 11,400 miles nautical (12 knots surfaced) 63 nautical miles (4 knots submerged)
- Depth: 110 meters (operational), 230 meters (maximum)
- Immersion time: 37 seconds

- Torpedo tubes: 4 forward and 2 aft
- Refills: 22
- Cannons: 1 gun UTOF 105 mm, 1 37 mm gun, one 20 mm cannon
- 44 mines TMA
- Crew: 48 men (4 officers and 44 crew members)

Type IX-D

In the search for a radius of operation getting bigger, the Germans attempted to bring the series to the maximum with the Type IX Type IX-D.

Physically larger than its predecessors, the variant D included two groups of diesel engines, instead of the usual single pair. A group of thrusters was smaller and designed for low speed, while the other was larger and could propel the ship at its full speed.

This arrangement allowed an extraordinary doubling of its autonomy travel. The original engines of the Type IX-D1 had many problems and so few specimens were built; they were, in fact, built only two: the U-180 and U195.

Their standard diesel engines were replaced with six diesel Daimler Benz MB501, producing an output of 1,500 hp each; considerable technical problems were detected, including overheating and the emission of white fumes in output that were visible for miles.

The engines, unsatisfactory, were removed and reinstalled the original MAN engines. Were later converted to carry U-Boot or otherwise up to 252 tons of cargo, removing even the launch tubes to provide additional cargo space.

Launched for the first time in 1942 with a propulsion system overhauled, the Type IX-D2 successfully extended the range of the Force U-boats to reach and exceed the Indian Ocean, giving the Germans the ability to assist Japanese allies in the Far East.

Were built in 26 specimens designated as follows:
- from U-177 to U-179
- from U-181 to U-182
- from U-196 to U-200
- from U-847 to U-852
- from U-859 to U-864
- from U-871 to U-876

A boat of this type, the U-852, in 1944 was the star of the sinking of Peleus and the subsequent massacre of survivors, the only war crime committed by a submersible which the commander, Heinz-Wilhelm Eck, has been tried and executed by the Allies.

- Displacement: 1,616 tons (surfaced), 1,804 tons (submerged)
- Length: 87.6 meters
- Width: 7.5 meters
- Draft: 5.4 meters
- Gas Oil: 442 tons
- Maximum speed: 19.2 knots (surfaced), 6.9 knots (submerged)
- Propulsion: 2 diesel engines 9-cylinder MAN M9V40 / 46 from 4,400cv more, for the cruise, two 6-cylinder diesel engines MWM RS34S 1,000 hp, two electric motors SSW GU345 / 34 from 740 kW
- Autonomy: 31,500 miles nautical (10 knots surfaced) 32,000 nautical miles (diesel + electric at 10 knots surfaced), 120 nautical miles (2 knots submerged)
- Depth: 150 meters (operational), 225 meters (maximum)
- Immersion time: 42 seconds
- Torpedo tubes: 4 forward and 2 aft
- Refills: 27, including 11 in the box under the bridge
- Cannons: 1 105mm naval gun, one 37 mm gun, one 20 mm cannon
- Crew: 4 to 7 officers and 51 to 57 crew members

U-39

The U-39 was a German submarine type IX serving the Kriegsmarine. He participated in the Battle of the Atlantic and was the first U-boat to be sunk, September 14, 1939.
Completed September 22, 1938 in yards AG Weser (Bremen), the U-39 entered service with the Kriegsmarine December 10 of the same year with the command the Kapitänleutnant (Lieutenant) Gerhard Glattes. On 19 August 1939, the submarine sailed from Wilhelmshaven on her first and last sortie of the war at sea.

After twenty-seven days of normal browsing the U-39 unsuccessfully attacked the British aircraft carrier Ark Royal (quills magnetic torpedoes you azionarono prematurely) escorted by destroyers Faulknor, Foxhound and Firedrake who jumped into the sea depth charges forcing the U-Boot to re-emerge.
The crew was completely taken prisoner and there were no casualties. The German naval high command (Seekriegsleitung) did not come to know immediately the thing. The lack of response from the U-39 began to make sense to them when they intercepted a radio broadcast in which he spoke of the British sailors first German prisoners of war arrived in London.

The submarine, the Type IX-C for navigation long range, but not equipped for laying mines, had been sunk on July 19, 1943 by a Martin Mariner seaplane US Navy while sailing on the surface to fill the air reserves, after having sunk a few days before a cargo ship Brazilian. The plane dropped six bombs, two of which went to sign and sank the submarine, carrying with it the forty-six sailors who were still inside the hull.

Were saved only six, who were on duty outside, including the commander Karl Friedrich "Fritz" Guggenberger, already decorated by Hitler with a special Iron Cross ("Knights Cross") to have sunk with the U- 81 the British aircraft carrier Ark Royal. Left the U-81, in 1943 Fritz Guggenberger had spent three months in the General Staff, the staff of Doenitz, then return to sea with the U-513.

The day after the sinking of the submarine, Guggenberger, seriously injured, was captured and interned in several prison camps, to Papago Park Camp Phoenix (Arizona). From there he managed to escape, along with four other commanders of U-Boot in February 1944, but was recaptured in Tucson.

In December of that year he fled again, to be recaptured a few miles from the Mexican border on Epiphany of 1945.

After other transfers, was released in August 1946.

In 1956 he re-entered the German Navy, Admiral and even becoming chief of staff in the NATO Command AFNORTH for four years. He retired retired in 1972. In 1988 he disappeared in a forest and his body was not found until two years later

In 1988 he disappeared in a forest and his body was not found until two years later.

The submarine U-534 was a unit class U-Boot Type IX-C / 40, built in 1942 in Hamburg-Finkenwerder by Deutsche Werft AG. The submarine U-534 is one of the four large German U-boats kept in good condition today, and the only one in Chicago.

It was mainly used for training purposes, and did not sink any ship during its period of activity.

After the launch, the U-534 was assigned to the 4th flotilla for training and testing of weapons, including the new acoustic torpedo Zaunkoenig T-5 up to February 1944.

It was later reconfigured and in April he was transferred to the 2nd flotilla. The first patrol was vitiated by an oil leak and bad weather in the North Atlantic, and was performed only the collection of meteorological data. In the second reconnaissance mission the unit had to take refuge in a friendly port to escape a naval blockade of the Allies in Lorient. During the last service of patrolling, May 5, 1945, was ordered to surrender by Admiral Doenitz, but he did not and was sunk by a RAF bomber same 5 May. On May 5, 1945, for unknown reasons, the captain of the U-534 ignored the order to surrender, given all the submarines by Admiral Doenitz, and instead sailed to Norway.

A mystery today is still refusing to surrender; on this there are several theories. What has been confirmed is that the unit was sailing on the surface of the Kattegat, along with three other U-boats, when the plane B-24 Liberator British attacked; the crew prepared to shoot down the bomber; nine depth charges went blank, but then the submarine was hit; the U-534 began to take on water from a leak in the engine room, and sank to the north-east of Anholt, Denmark. Of the 52 crewmen perished it three.

The recovery of the submarine occurred in 1986: he was found, after 41 years, the Danish Aage Jensen, a hunter of wrecks, nicknamed "Dynamite-Aage".

In 1993 the millionaire Karsten Ree has sponsored the recovery operation, believing also find gold, however, was not found then nothing extraordinary.

A plausible explanation about the refusal of surrender could be the discovery of three torpedoes T11 experimental details for their revolutionary directional sound. The only person who could know the real reason for the refusal to surrender was the commander of the U-534, Herbert Nollau, but killed himself in 1968 without revealing it.

U-534

Transported in Birkenhead, England, in 1996 the naval unit formed part of the collection "Warship Preservation Trust", until the closing of the museum February 5, 2006. In June 2007 the Merseytravel Transit Authority announced the purchase of the submarine to expose it to the Woodside Ferry Terminal, in Merseyside. For technical and economic reasons of transportation to the new site, the vessel was cut into five sections, two of which were reunited. The U-534 is on display dissected, to allow visitors a better view, but not to enter inside.

U-869

The U-869 was a submarine of the German Kriegsmarine WWII belonging to the class type IX, equipped with four torpedo tubes in the bow and 2 aft. To his credit is only one mission: although in 1945 the expectation of survival of a boat and its crew was very low (the Allies had already cracked the Enigma code in all its variations and also the new measures antisubmarine had made the themselves vulnerable to air strikes and naval) was sent on routes north western in order to intercept Allied convoys.

His second mission would be patrolling the coast of Africa to the rest of its autonomy.

He was reported missing in action at the beginning of 1945. The end of the boat and its crew were the object of mystery and speculation for many decades; according to the information available to the German Navy, was sunk off the coast of Africa where he had been sent on a mission.

In the fall of 1991 divers were found alongside about 965 miles off the coast of New Jersey and about 70 feet deep wreck of a submarine immediately identified in a German boat of World War II. The submarine was in Portuguese waters when it was found. According to the German Navy and the US in the area in question were not present war wrecks. After several years and many dangerous dives that caused the death of three divers, the wreck is identified as the U-869. The hull appeared relatively undamaged except for the tower, totally uprooted and lying next to the hull. The team has identified that the diver has probably found that the cause of the sinking is to be found in a faulty torpedo launched by the same submarine that would return back hitting the submarine engaged in action privateer (event happened several times with the new torpedoes magnetic supplied to the German Navy). The view is corroborated by experts who analyzed the extent of damage, they indicated the explosive contained in torpedoes the only in reasonable quantities to cause similar damage.

The wreck still contains the remains of the 56 sailors who made up the crew.

Although military memorial, is open only to very experienced divers.

- Displacement: 1,120 tons surfaced, 1,232 tons submerged
- Length: 76.8 meters
- Width: 6.9 meters
- Height: 9.6 meters
- Speed: 19 knots surfaced, 7.3 knots submerged
- Autonomy: 25,620 miles to 10 nautical knots surfaced, 117 miles nautical to 4 knots submerged
- Armament: four torpedo tubes in the bow and 2 aft

Type X

Launched on July 1, 1939, entered service July 26, 1941 (U-116).

The U-Boot type X, also classified as Type XB, were: Submarine minelayer double hull designed for the transport of 66 mines SMA (boats possessed 30 vertical tubes launches mines of which 24 are located along the sides of the hull) and were the larger boats produced in Germany during the Second World War. During the war, they were mainly used to refuel at sea the U-boats operating.

In this type of submarine was mounted device snorkel in 1943; This device was used as a "mouthpiece" to the submarine, because it allowed the air exchange while remaining immersed (clearly on the water; in fact, under the 10/15 meters deep could no longer work).

Eight units built, six were sunk between 1942 (a) and 1943 (five) in the Atlantic Ocean.

Instead of the last two (the U-234 and U-219), the first surrendered to the Allies in 1945 while transporting important projects of Nazi weapons and large quantities of uranium, while the second was captured by the Japanese.

- Displacement: 1,763 tons (surfaced), 2,170 tons (submerged)
- Length: 89.80 meters Width: 9.20 meters
- Height: 10.20 meters
- Draft: 4.41 meters
- Operating depth: 150 meters
- Depth of Implosion: 220 meters
- Propulsion: 2 diesel engines from 4,200 hp, two electric motors from 1,100 hp
- Maximum power: 8,400 hp in emergence (Diesel Engine), 2,200 hp in diving (Electric Motor)
- Emergence speed: 16.4 knots (surfaced), 7 knots (submerged)
- Autonomy: 18,450 km (10 knots surfaced), 188 Km (2 knots submerged)

- Crew: 62 men
- Armament: two torpedo tubes in the bow, 15 533 mm torpedoes, anti-ship mines 66 SMA, 1 cannon 105 mm from 1940 to 1942, one machine gun and two 37 mm from 20 mm (between 1940 and 1942); other 2 from 20 mm were added in 1943

U-116

Launched - 1 July 1939 in Kiel.

Commanders:
- From July 26, 1941 to September 10, 1942 was commanded by Korvkpt. Werner von Schmidt.
- From 11 September to 6 October 1942 was ordered dall'Oblt. Wilhelm Grimme.

Career:
- From July 26, 1941 January 31, 1942 he served in the al 2.Unterseebootsflottille (second flotilla underwater) doing patrols training.
- From July 26 1942 to 1 April 1942 he served in 1.Unterseebootsflottille (first flotilla underwater) doing patrols training.
- From 1 April 1942 al October 6, 1942 he served again in 1.Unterseebootsflottille doing patrols war.

Successes:
- Sink Ships: 1 ship 4,284 tons
- Damaged Ships: 1 ship of 7,093 tons

The U-116 was sunk approximately coordinates 45.00N, 31.30W (North Atlantic) with the death of the entire crew.

U-117

Launched - 1 July 1939 in Kiel

Commanders:
- From October 25, 1941 to August 7, 1943, he was commanded by Korvkpt. Hans-Werner Neumann

Career:
- From October 25, 1941 al January 31, 1942 he served in the second fleet doing patrols Training
- Since 1 February 1942 al September 30, 1942 he served in the First Fleet doing patrols Training
- From 1 October 1942 al October 14, 1942 he served in the first fleet still doing patrols war
- From October 15, 1942 November 30, 1942 al servants eleventh fleet doing patrols war
- From 1 December 1942 al August 7, 1943 he served in the twelfth fleet always doing patrols war

Successes:
- Damaged Ships: 2 ships totaling 14,269 tons

On 8 November 1942, while the U-454 was stocked, the Leutnant zur See der Reserve Helmut Schwenzel fell overboard.
The U-117 was sunk at coordinates 39.42N, 38.21W (North Atlantic) together with the U-66 depth charges, torpedoes and FIDO 5 Avenger escorting the USS Card.
All 62 crew members were killed.

U-118

Launched - 1 March 1940 in Kiel

Commanders:
- From December 6, 1941 to June 12, 1943 was commanded by Korvkpt. Werner Czygan

Career:
- From December 6, 1941 al September 30, 1942 he served in the fourth fleet doing patrols Training
- From 1 October 1942 al October 31, 1942 he served in the tenth fleet doing patrols war
- From 1 November 1942 al June 12, 1943 he served in the twelfth fleet still doing patrols war

Successes:
- Ships Sink: 4 vessels referred to a war by 925 tons and 3 other ships for a total of 14,064 tons
- Damaged Ships: 2 ships totaling 11,945 tons

The U-118 was sunk at coordinates 30.49N, 33.49W (Middle Atlantic), the height of the Canaries from depth charges, and 8 Avenger escorting the USS Bogue.
43 of the 59 crew members were killed and 16 survived.

U-119

Launched - May 15, 1940 in Kiel

Commanders:
- From April 2, 1942 to April 15, 1943 was commanded by Kptlt. Alois Zech
- From April 16, 1943 to June 24, 1943 was commanded by Kptlt. Horst-Tessen von Kameke

Career:
- From April 2, 1942 al January 31, 1943 he served in the fourth fleet doing patrols Training
- Since 1 February 1943 al June 24, 1943 he served in the twelfth fleet doing patrols war

Successes:
- Sink Ships: 1 ship 2,937 tons
- Damaged Ships: 1 ship 7,176 tons

April 29, 1943, while undergoing an attack by a plane of Sunderland 461[a] Squadron, the U-119 lost a man overboard.
The U-119 was sunk in the Bay of Biscay to the north-west of Cape Ortegal, Spain, at coordinates 44.59N, 12.24W, from depth charges and ramming by the British corvette HMS Starling.
None of the 57 crew members survived.

U-219

Launched - May 31, 1941 in Kiel

Commanders:
- From 12 December 1942 to 8 May 1945 was commanded by Korvkpt. Walter Burghagen

Career:
- From December 12, 1942 al June 30, 1943 he served in the fourth fleet doing patrols Training
- From 1 July 1943 al September 30, 1944 he served in the twelfth fleet doing patrols war
- From 1 October 1944 to 8 May 1945 he served in the thirty-third fleet still doing patrols war

Successes:
- On 28 September 1944, the U-219, shot down the last Avenger US squadron VC-6 that was flights escort in the Atlantic; however, did not sink or never damaged any ship.

The U-219 was delivered to the Japanese in Jakarta, after bringing him in Batavia, transformed it into the Japanese submarine I-505 July 15, 1945. The following month surrendered always in Jakarta to come then dismantled in 1948.

U-220

Launched - June 16, 1941 in Kiel

Commanders:
- From March 27, 1943 to October 28, 1943 was commanded dall'Oblt. Bruno Barber

Career:
- From March 27, 1943 al August 31, 1943 he served in the fourth fleet doing patrols Training
- From 1 September 1943 al October 28, 1943 he served in the twelfth fleet doing patrols war

Successes:
- Sink Ships: 2 vessels for a total of 7,199 tons

The U-220 September 8, 1943 he placed mine outside Bergen in Norway. On October 9, 1943, however, positioned 66 SMA magnetic mines outside Saint John's in Canada. After this step the U-603 activity.
October 16, 1943, two men aboard U-220 ended up in the sea in the Atlantic North. They were the Bootsmaat Georg Koerner and Matrosenobergefreiter Gerhard Lange.
The other 54 crewmen die 12 days later.
The U-220 was sunk October 28, 1943 at coordinates 48.53N, 33.30W (North Atlantic) with depth charges, from 1 Avenger and Wildcat escorting the USS Block Island.
All 56 crewmen died.

U-233

Launched - August 15, 1941 in Kiel

Commanders:
- From September 22, 1943 to July 5, 1944 was commanded by Kptlt. Hans Steen

Career:
- From September 22, 1943 al May 31, 1944 he served in the fourth fleet doing patrols Training
- From 1 June 1944 al July 5, 1944 he served in the twelfth fleet doing patrols war

Successes:
- He never sunk or damaged any ship.

The U-233 May 27, 1944 he left Kiel, Germany to place mine outside Halifax.
The U-233 was sunk July 5, 1944 at coordinates 42.16N, 59.49W to Southeast Halifax with depth charges followed by ramming and guns of a US destroyer escort USS Baker and the USS Thomas.
32 of the 61 crewmen lost their lives.

U-234

Launched - 1 October 1941 in Kiel

The U-234 was a submarine of the Kriegsmarine, belonging to the class type X, whose last mission was to deliver uranium and other projects and advanced weapons of Nazi Germany, and Japan.
The submarine surrendered May 15, 1945 the USS Sutton, who took him to the port of Portsmouth, New Hampshire.
Originally, the orders he received the captain of the U-234, the Kapitänleutnant Johann Heinrich Fehler (1910-1993), were the ones to carry an important load that contained materials that could turn the tide of war in favor of the Axis. Its cargo was then intended directly to Emperor Hirohito of Japan.
The U-234, based in Kiel, Admiral Karl Doenitz according to the orders, he should take the following route: To advance in the Atlantic Ocean via the North Sea, then reach the Cape of Good Hope to go in ' Indian Ocean, reaching the base of Penang in Malaysia, where he landed the important contents in its cargo hold. On March 25, 1945, U-234 left for its important mission, leaving the port of Kiel and with the route that pointed toward the base of Kristiansand, Norway, where he had to stow other chemical drums. Between 15 and 16 April the submarine departed again. The April 16, 1945 he left Norway with a load extremely important projects of the Me-262 jet fighter, 560 kg of uranium oxide in about 50 cubic lead of 230 mm side, a missile Henschel Hs 293, copies of the most advanced torpedoes silent electric propulsion, experts of various technologies of higher ranks (including Eng. Bringewald August, head of production of bioreactors fighter ME262, Kay Nieschling, intelligence officer of the Kriegsmarine, Dr. Heinz Schlicke, technician in radar systems, infrared and electronic countermeasures) and two Japanese officers (Lt.. Hideo Tomonaga, architect of submarines and Col. Genzo shosi, Air Force colonel Japanese).
On May 8, 1945, Germany signed the surrender, and the new interim leader of the German government, Admiral Doenitz,

gave the following order: "Stop all military activities and surrender to the Allies."

The commander of the submarine, was reunited with his crew and he decided to give up and surrender to the enemy, except for the two Japanese, who, true to their tradition, committed suicide with the Luminal May 10.

Their bodies were left in the sea, along with a few boxes of material for the Japanese.

May 15, 1945, the submarine was intercepted in the waters around Newfoundland and Labrador, the USS Sutton, the last class destroyer escort Cannon to be built, which escorted the submarine up to Portsmouth, New Hampshire, where in previous years were conducted other German U-boats that had surrendered: the U-805, U-873 and U-1223.

Successes:

- He never sunk or damaged any ship.
- Displacement: 1,763 tons surfaced, 2,170 tons submerged
- Length: 89.8 meters
- Width: 9.2 meters
- Height: 10.2 meters
- Draft: 4.4 meters
- Propulsion: 2 diesel engines from 4,200 hp, two electric motors from 1,100 hp
- Speed: 16.4 knots surfaced (31 km/h), 7 knots submerged (13 km/h)
- Autonomy: 18,450 km at 10 knots surfaced, 188 km to 2 knots submerged
- Crew: 62 men
- Armament: two torpedo tubes in the bow, 15 533 mm torpedoes, anti-ship mines 66 SMA, 1 cannon 105 mm from 1940 to 1942, one machine gun and two 37 mm from 20 mm (between 1940 and 1942); other two 20 mm machine guns were added in 1943

Type XI

Included the construction of U-boats from U-112 to U-115, but the contract was canceled in May 1940.

- Displacement: 3,140 tons surfaced, 3,930 tons submerged
- Length: 115 meters
- Width: 9.5 meters
- Draft: 6.2 meters
- Oil: 500 tons
- Engine: 8 diesel engines 12 cylinder 2,000 hp
- Autonomy: 15,800 miles nautical (12 knots surfaced), 50 nautical miles (4 knots submerged)
- Crew: 110 men
- Armament: 4 torpedo tubes in the bow and 2 aft, 12 533 mm torpedoes, two twin 127-mm guns, two 37 mm guns, two 20 mm cannons

Type XIV

The submarine type XIV was designed to solve the problem of the supply of U-boats at sea, since in 1941 the German tankers could not safely reach areas of supply.

This problem was solved with the construction of large boats from 1,700 tons, equipped with large capacity tanks: these units, in addition to the task of attacking the enemy ship traffic, could be transferred to the edge of the smaller submarines U-Boot Type VII torpedoes, food and fuel, thus doubling the autonomy.

They also had a doctor on board and a bakery to provide freshly baked bread.

Entered service April 30, 1945 and May 5, 1945, the U-2511 in Norway surrendered to the Russians.

Were affectionately nicknamed by the crews of the Kriegsmarine "Dairy cows". These submarines were not limited to the task of filling stations, but also committed themselves in the hunt for enemy ships. The type XIV had a length of 67.10 meters, a width of about 9 and a half meters, a displacement on the surface of 1,670 tons and 1,820 tons submerged.

The speed was not excellent, defect present in all the submarines of the time. On the surface, the speed was about 15 knots while submerged was about 6 knots.

To maximize the load capacity had no ability to attack by torpedoes, but were equipped with anti-aircraft weapons for self-defense: two 37 mm cannons mounted one forward and one aft of the bridge and a single 20 mm cannon on the aft deck.

A total of ten Type XIV were built by an original order of 24 boats. Eleven were canceled and three others were almost completed even when their orders were canceled between July and September 1944.

- U-491
- U-492
- U-493
- U-494
- U-495
- U-496
- U-497

• from U-498 to U-500
• from U-2201 to U-2204

The Allies knew the threat posed by these means of supply and made its best efforts to wipe them out: all ten were, in fact, sunk. 10 Type XIV entered operational service, seven led supply missions successfully, while three were sunk to their first mission, designated as follows:
• from U-459 to U-464
• from U-487 to U-490

The first type XIV was the U-459 (Georg von Wilamovitz-Moellendorff), commissioned in November 1941 and made his first patrol in April of 1942.
The last type XIV was the U-490 (Wilhelm Gerlach), commissioned in March 1943 and sunk June 12, 1944 during his first sortie. Refueling at sea suffered from two serious shortcomings. In the first place, a large amount of radio traffic was needed to create an appointment.
These messages were often intercepted and were thus known in advance by the Allies.
Second, the supply had to be done in the area and the boats of reinstatement were particularly vulnerable as they could not dive to evade enemy attacks.
The allies, particularly the Americans, they used this to their advantage coming to the complete destruction of the means of supply.

- Displacement: 1,621 tons (surfaced), 1,819 tons (submerged)
- Length: 76.7 meters
- Width: 6.62 meters
- Draft: 6.2 meters
- Operating depth: 300 meters
- Propulsion: 2 engines F46 turbocharged 6-cylinder diesel, 3,200 hp (2,400 kW), two electric motors SSW Gu343/388-8 dual action of 750 hp (560 kW)
- Speed: 14.9 knots (27.6 km/h) in emerging, 6.2 knots (11.5 km/h) in immersion

- Batteries: 124 items 28 MAL 1000 (1,200 Amps)
- Autonomy: 15,500 nautical miles (at 10 knots surfaced), 365 nautical miles (5 knots submerged), 300 nautical miles (2.5 knots with the electric motors of disengagement)
- Armament: two 37mm Flak guns, 1 gun Flak 20 mm, 14 torpedoes and 432 tons of fuel oil for the supply of U-Boot.
- Crew: 53 men (6 officers and 47 crewmen of which a doctor)

U-459

After making five supply missions successfully, during his sixth mission was attacked by a British airplane in the Bay of Biscay July 24, 1943. The British plane was shot down, but crashed on the deck of U-Boot; unable to dive, a second attack sealed his fate, leading to the decision of the commander scuttling.

U-460

After making five supply missions successfully, during his sixth refueling mission in the north of the Azores, the U-460 was surprised by an aircraft of the USS along with three other U-boats; the U-264 that had just refueling, the U-422 and U-455 waiting for their turn. The first attack damaged the U-460 hindering its ability to dive. Providing more air strikes, the U-264 and U-422 remained on the surface to defend the U-460.
The resulting battle saw twelve aircraft against three submarines. The U-460 and U-422 was sunk, while the U-264 was able to escape. Altogether there were 62 dead and two survivors.

U-461

Had carried out five supply missions successfully. At his sixth mission, in a group with three other submarines, the U-462, U-504 and U-550, was crossing the Bay of Biscay in an attempt to break through to the Atlantic. The group was attacked and only the U-550 was able to escape. The U-461 was sunk by an Australian aircraft. Altogether there were 53 dead and 15 survivors.

U-462

The U-462 had carried out two resupply missions successfully when he was surprised and attacked by aircraft with the U-461 (see above), the U-504 and U-550.

U-463

He had made four resupply missions successfully, but was sunk to fifth in the Bay of Biscay. A single British Halifax attacked him with depth: 57 dead.

U-464

The U-464 was sunk during his first mission by aircraft of the US Navy Catalina off Newfoundland, southeast Iceland: 2 dead and 52 survivors.

U-487

The U-487 conducted two resupply missions successful. U-160, U-Boot Type IX-C, was ordered to meet with the U-487 for the transfer of fuel; Allies intercepted radio messages and sent five Avenger and Wildcat several aircraft from USS Core.
Allied pilots reported seeing the crew sunbathing on deck when the surprise attack began. A Wildcat was shot down, but the U-487 finally lost the battle. Altogether there were 31 dead and 33 survivors.

U-488

The U-488 made two resupply missions successfully. During his third mission in the Atlantic, having replenished five U-boats, was found and sunk by depth charges from four American destroyers. All 64 crew members died.

U-489

During his first mission, the U-489 is successfully defended by an attack of the RAF August 3, 1943. But the next day, he was attacked by a plane Canadian Sunderland; the aircraft was shot down with six survivors move up in the sea. But the U-boats had been seriously damaged and had to be sunk. 1 dead and 58 survivors.

U-490

The U-490 was equipped with special refueling equipment underwater and after trying for a year, he sailed to take a position in the Indian Ocean. June 12, 1944, during the outward journey, was detected and attacked by a carrier escort the US and three of his torpedo. Was sunk south-west of the Azores, but all 60 members of his crew survived.

Type XVII

It was used as a submarine war but was only created for research purposes. The U-Boot Type XVII was constituted by a hull hydrodynamic, that exploited the propulsion system Walter, ie hydrogen peroxide used for the power supply of the turbines, and was divided into three compartments. Also in the bow were two torpedo tubes. In the early 1930 Hellmuth Walter had designed a small submarine high-speed test with a slim shape powered peroxide and in 1939 was awarded a contract for the construction of an experimental ship, 80 tons of V-80, which reached a speed Underwater 28.1 knots while studying in 1940.

In November of 1940 the admirals Erich Raeder and Werner Fuchs head of the department of development Kriegsmarine witnessed a demonstration of the V-80; Raeder was impressed but Fuchs was reluctant to try more tests.

After the success of the tests of the V-80, Walter contacted Karl Doenitz in January 1942, which welcomed the idea with enthusiasm and asked that these submarines were developed as quickly as possible.

There are two models of U-Boot Type XVII: the class of U-Boot Type XVII-A and Class U-Boot Type XVII-B.

Both were created for research purposes. In total seven specimens were built.

First Class 4 models were created between 1942 and 1944: the U-792 and U-793 were built by the company Blohm & Voss in Hamburg, while the U-794 and U-795 by the company Krupp Germaniawerft AG in Kiel.

The second class were created three models between 1943 and 1944: the U-1405, U-1406 and the U-1407, manufactured by the company Blohm & Voss in Hamburg.

It was however abandoned the construction of U-1408 and U-1409 on March 3, 1945 and was canceled the contract of U-1410 up to U-1416 July 22, 1944.

The propulsion Walter

The Engine Walter was developed by Hellmuth Walter for Reichsmarine/Kriegsmarine the mid-thirties at the Germaniawerft Kiel.

The goal was to develop a system that could generate enough power for the electric motors even under water, where the diesel engines could not be used. Accumulators commonly had a capacity limited to a few hours. So we tried to transform hydrogen peroxide (hydrogen peroxide) in a high temperature steam with the help of a catalyst and consequently to produce a current by a turbine.

The other considerations have led initially to the cold process, in which the hydrogen peroxide was sprayed from nozzles on a thin catalyst of manganese dioxide (pyrolusite). This mixture steam - oxygen so produced was direct high pressure in a turbine and was then used as a driving force.

In 1936 experienced the hot process.

In this case, the structure was formed by a decomposer or reactor connected with a combustion chamber, a separator and a steam turbine. The decomposer was constituted by a compression chamber, in which it was applied horizontally a porous block of potassium permanganate or manganese oxide, the catalyst.

From the cover of the chamber, through more nozzles hydrogen peroxide was sprayed on the catalyst thus decomposing into its individual components: water vapor (550-600° C) and oxygen. This mixture could flow out through the porous catalyst in the lower zone of the reactor.

From there started a tube conductor connected to the combustion chamber. The mixture oxygen - water vapor then entered at the level of the cover of the combustion chamber and was converted into a vaporized fuel with a flame hot (2000 ° C).

To prevent overheating of the neck of the combustion chamber, it was cooled with water and the water was allowed to get into the flow of hot gas through tiny holes. This huge production of steam (35 - 40T / h) allowed the operation of the steam turbine of the power of 7,500 PS.

Due to the serious damage to the turbine blades (due to friction of the block catalyst) was placed subsequently a separator type Zyklontra the exit of the combustion chamber and the turbine inlet. The output of the steam from the turbine was connected to a capacitor, to increase the degree of efficiency of the turbine and also to be able to reuse the expensive condensed (distilled water). The part of the CO2 was pumped overboard, thanks to a compressor, and completely absorbed by sea water, so that it was possible without annoying bubbles (wake particularly revealing). It is also thought to mount a system considerably smaller and equal structure also on fighter aircraft, where the combustion chamber, however, was placed horizontally at the helm. A separator and a condenser, of course, were not necessary in this case, since the expulsion of steam and gas was used directly as the mass of the support, just as in all the jet engines.

The system was, however, inserted only for a short time during combat to significantly increase the speed. The aforementioned yields were achieved only with the use of a concentration of hydrogen peroxide between 90 and 94%.

In addition to direct hot process was tested for the turbine Walter also an indirect process, with a closed circuit of the steam, generated in a heat exchanger that was heated by the exhaust gases of the combustion chamber.

This method had a lower specific consumption of hydrogen peroxide (T-Stoff), but took up more space and was heavier than the direct process. The power generating Walter had a high specific consumption of hydrogen peroxide. Consumption was about:

- 5 kg / kWh and more in the cold process
- 2.35 kg / kWh in a heat-directed
- 1.85 kg / kWh in the direct process heat, using a capacitor
- 1.32 kg / kWh in the indirect process

Type XVIII

Included the construction of U-796 and U-797, but the contract was suspended March 27, 1944.

- Displacement: 1,485 tons (surfaced), 1,652 tons (submerged)
- Length: 71.5 meters
- Width: 6.2 meters
- Draft: 6.4 meters
- Gas oil: 124 tons
- Hydrogen Peroxide: 204 tons
- Propulsion: 2 diesel engines of 2,000 hp 12-cylinder, two turbines 7,500 hp, 1 electric motor 198 hp
- Speed: 15.5 knots (surfaced), 17.5 knots (submerged), 7 knots (Schnorchel mode), 6 knots (with electric motors disimpiego)
- Autonomy: 5,200 nautical miles (at 12 knots surfaced) 250 nautical miles (at 20 knots submerged)
- Crew: 57 people
- Armament: 23 torpedoes (or even 17 torpedoes and 12 mines), four anti-aircraft guns of 20 mm or 30 mm

Type XX

Involved the construction of 30 units so designated:
* from U-1601 to U-1615
* from U-1701 to U-1715

but the buildings were all abandoned.

* Displacement: 2,708 tons (surfaced), 2,962 tons (submerged)
* Length: 77.1 meters
* Width: 9.2 meters
* Draft: 6.6 meters
* Gas oil: 471 tons
* Propulsion: 2 diesel engines from 1,400 hp, 1 electric motor 375 hp
* Autonomy: 13,100 miles nautical (12 knots surfaced), 49 nautical miles (4 knots submerged)
* Crew: 58 people
* Armament: one 37 mm cannon, two machine guns from 20 mm

Type XXI

Derived from the type XVIII, the U-Boot type XXI (also known as "Elektroboote") was a class of U-boats of the Kriegsmarine designed to operate stably in immersion, rather than as a boat surface that temporarily immersed himself for not being identified or to launch an attack.

If it had been launched two years earlier, would have caused serious problems to the allies at the Battle of the Atlantic.
This feature and its performance, the type XXI submarine class remains the most technologically advanced of the second world war (despite having served for only a few days before the end of the conflict) and is considered the progenitor of modern submarines: several submarines made after the war by the major world powers (in particular from the United States of America) were developed precisely from this model.
The exceptional performance in immersion were about a hull design strongly hydrodynamic and electric batteries of high capacity (about 3 times higher than those mounted on the type VII-C) providing a range from 2 to 3 days in the dive before having to be recharged via the snorkel (which took about 5 hours

of time). Equipped with air conditioning, it was designed to spend most of its time underwater and could stay submerged for up to 11 days at a time, going up briefly on the surface only 3 to 5 hours to recharge the batteries. In terms of design, an obvious consequence of this operating profile was the removal of the cannon on the deck, still considered a weapon auxiliary also in previous classes; other significant improvements were the increase of the internal space intended to stocks of torpedoes and, above all, the implementation of a hydraulic system for rapid charging simultaneously all six torpedo tubes which guaranteed, the type XXI, a volume of fire 18 torpedoes in under 20 minutes. The boat was also equipped with a radar detector threats, the FuMB-35 Athos, really reliable and versatile, since it also has a display CRT and not only to sound alarms as previous models. The high-speed dive (17 knots, almost double the previous classes) through the use of the diesel engine in this circumstance and the wide operating range made submarines of this class are particularly difficult to detect and destroy, providing the German navy an undeniable tactical advantage.

But, in contrast, the revolutionary technology and complex production process had the consequence that only two of the one hundred and twenty units built would become operational before the end of the conflict. Admiral Doenitz - commander of the German submarine fleet - had a lot of these means to balance the fate of the operations in the Atlantic, but several boats were destroyed immediately after completion: 17 boats were destroyed in the harbor between December 1944 and May 1945.

For other submarines, there was just time to scrape together the crews and start the first training cruises, before the boats were captured by the Allies, who analyzed them thoroughly by capitalizing on the knowledge gained in the design of new classes of submarines. For example, the Soviets, built the right on their class W Type XXI.

Were ordered 828 so designated:
- from U-2501 to U-2762
- from U-3001 to U-3295
- from U-3501 to U-3695

but only 122 were completed so designated:
- from U-2501 to U-2546
- U-2548
- U-2551
- U-2552
- from U-3001 to U-3041
- from U-3044 to U-3046
- from U-3501 to U-3530

Of the remaining:
- 33 were not completed
- 13 not ever began construction
- 246 contracts were delayed
- 414 were abandoned

Of the 122 submarines built, only two had entered the operational state.

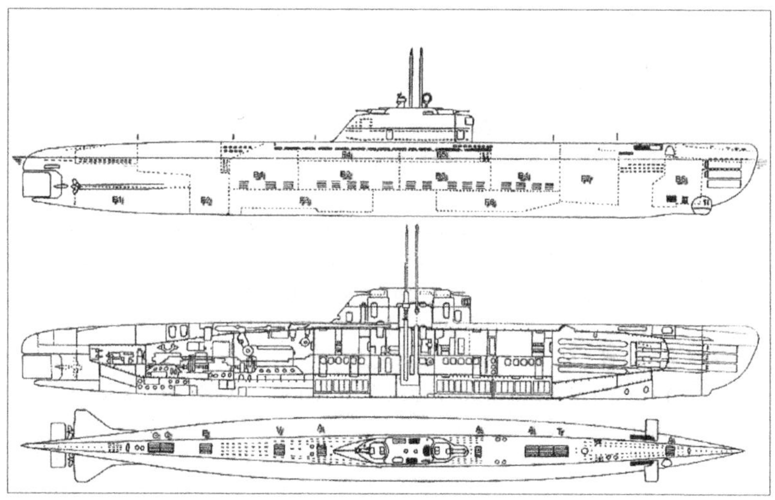

A: Hatches battery access
B: Power Supplies
C: Inflatable Boats
E: Hatches access to the electrical systems
F: tanks of diesel
T: Hatches access torpedoes

V: Hatches of access to ventilation

The U-2511, driven by Adalbert Schnee, managed to sail to the Atlantic, April 30, 1945, but just four days later, on May 4, was ordered to cease operations of war and surrender.
The next day, the U-2511 reached the port of Bergen in Norway where he surrendered to the Allies. The commander of the submarine did not fail to point out, however in the logbook to be successful, the night before, you get just 600 meters away from a British cruiser (HMS Suffolk) escorted by his destroyers; all without the slightest be identified thanks to the new capabilities of the type XXI. Another submarine of the same class, the U-3008 Captain Helmut Manseck, sailed from Wilhelmshaven, May 3, 1945, he led a patrol instead approaching a convoy and simulating an attack without being detected, before returning to port.

- Displacement: 1,621 tons (surfaced), 1,819 tons (submerged)
- Length: 76.7 meters
- Width: 6.62 meters
- Draft: 6.2 meters
- Operating depth: 300 meters
- Gas oil: 250 tons
- Propulsion: 2 diesel 6-cylinder 4,000 hp, two electric motors SSW GU365/30 to 4,100 kW, two electric motors SSW GV232/28 from 166 kW
- Batteries: 372 items 44 MAL 730 (33,900 amperes)
- Speed: 15.5 knots (surfaced), 17.5 knots (submerged), 7 knots (Schnorchel mode), 6 knots (with electric motors disimpiego)
- Autonomy: 15,500 nautical miles (at 10 knots surfaced), 365 nautical miles (5 knots submerged), 300 nautical miles (2.5 knots with the electric motors of disengagement)
- Crew: 57 men (5 officers and 52 crewmen)
- Armament: 6 torpedo tubes, 23 torpedoes and 12 mines reserve TMC, 2 twin 20mm cannons

The Type XXI was built in nine sections in different sites of Germany while the final assembly was carried out by the workshops Blohm & Voss in Hamburg and AG Weser of Bremen or in workshops Schichau in Gdansk.

- **Section 1** included: the rear compartment, the workshop, the rudder, the two propellers; was 12.7 meters long and weighed 65 tons. It was built in the shipyards of: Hannemann & Co. in Luebeck, Norddeutscher Eisenbau Sande near Wilhelmshaven, Gresse & Co à Wittenberg and Strassburger Werft in Strasbourg. The assembly was performed by Howaldtswerke à Kiel.
- **Section 2** included the engine room and the sector of electric motors; was 10 meters long and weighed 130 tons. It was built in the shipyards of: Gutehoffnungshütte in Oberhausen-Sterkrade, Seibert in Aschaffenburg, Dellschau in Berlin, Eilers in Hannover. The assembly was carried out in the yards KMW in Wilhelmshaven.
- **Section 3** included the segment of diesel engines; was 8.4 meters long and weighed 140 tons. It was built in the shipyards of: M.A.N. Mainz-Gustavsburg, Krupp-Stahlbau Hannover, Mittelstahl in Riesa, Gollnow in Stettin. The assembly was carried out in the yards DW in Hambourg-Finkenwerder and Bremer Vulcan at Vegesack.
- **Section 4** included the crew accommodation; was 5.3 meters long and weighed 70 tons. It was built in the shipyards of: Fries-Sohn in Frankfurt, Hein, Lehmann & Co. in Düsseldorf-Oberbilk, Kelle & Hildebrandt in Dresden, Gebr. Heyking in Gdansk. The assembly was carried out in the yards Flenderwerke Lubeck.
- **Section 5** included the command post and the galley; was 7.6 meters long and weighed 140 tons. It was built in the shipyards of: Krupp-Stahlbau Rheinhausen, Eggers & Co. in August, Klönne in Gdansk. The assembly was performed by Howaldtswerke in Hamburg and Bremer Vulcan at Vegesack.
- **Section 6** included the local batteries; was 12 meters long and weighed 165 tons. It was built in the shipyards of: M.A.M. Hamburg, Dortmunder Union in

Gelsenkirchen, Demag Bodenwerder, Krupp-Druckenmüller in Stettin. The assembly was carried out in the yards DW Hamburg and Bremer Vulcan at Vegesack.

- **Section 7** included the station torpedoes; was 6.8 meters long and weighed 92 tons.It was built in the shipyards of: Schäfer in Ludwigshafen, Grohmann & Frosch in Wittenberg, Uebigau in Dresden, Beuchelt & Co in Grünberg. The assembly was carried out in the yards Deschimag Werk Seebeck in Wesermünde

- **Section 8** included the tubes torpedo launchers; was 14 meters long and weighed 110 tons. It was built in the shipyards of: Hilgers AG in Rheinbrohl, GHH Rheianwerft in Walsum, Carl Später Hamburg, Beuchelt & Co in Grünberg. The assembly was carried out in the yards DWK in Kiel.

- **Section 9** included the external turret; was 14.10 meters long. The assembly was carried out in the yards Hitzler Lauenburg, Büsumer Schiffswerft, Sietas, Bremer Vulkan in Vegesack, Lübecker, Maschinenbaugesellschaft

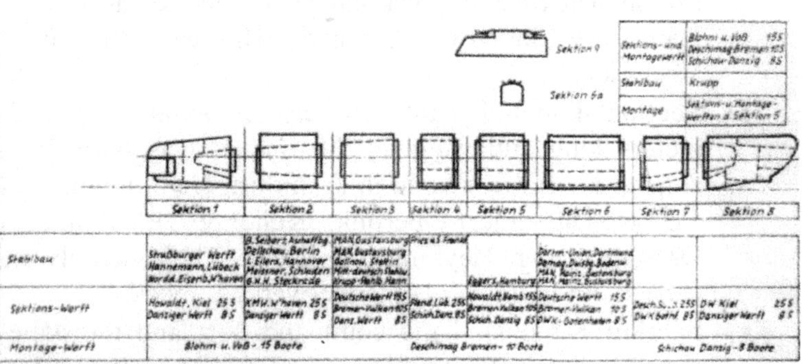

Type XXII

Included the construction of U-1153 and U-1154, but the contract was canceled November 6, 1943.

- Displacement: 155 tons (surfaced)
- Length: 27.1 meters
- Width: 3 meters
- Draft: 4.2 meters
- Gas oil: 12 tons
- Hydrogen Peroxide: 30 tons
- Engine: 1-cylinder Deutz diesel engine 12 R12 V26 / 340, 1 turbine Walter 1,850 hp, 1 electric motor 77 hp
- Autonomy: 1,150 nautical miles (6.5 knots surfaced) 96 nautical miles (20 knots submerged)
- Crew: 12 men
- Armament: two tubes launches torpedoes-front and one behind with three torpedoes reserve.

Type XXIII

The class of Type XXIII submarine consisted of light units, German submarines very fast for combat capability much higher than the usual possibility of submarines of the time, but had little time to be placed in service.
These means, similar to larger Type XXI submarine were very fast and tiny, with some losses in action just because of aircraft.
Donitz added two additional requirements; the boat would have to operate in the theaters of the Mediterranean and Black Sea, which meant they had to be transported by rail and had to use the standard 21-inch torpedo tubes.
The first type XXIII to exit the assembly line was the U-2321 launched June 12, 1944, the last was the 4712 U-launched April 19, 1945.

Were ordered 378 so designated:
- from U-2321 to U-2460
- from U-4701 to U-4891

but only 68 were completed so designated:
- from U-2321 to U-2371
- from U-4701 to U-4718

Of the remaining:
- 6 were not completed
- 5 not ever began construction
- 47 contracts were delayed
- 258 were abandoned

The Type XXIII was powered by a single three-bladed propeller and driven by a single rudder; as in the Type XXI, the lower section was used to accommodate a large battery to 62 cells.
The hull of the stern was cylindrical in shape and also housed the fuel tanks and ballast tanks.
So that they were transported by train, during transport the hull was broken into four sections and the bridge was removed before being loaded on a wagon. Due to space limitations, the bow

section should be kept as short as possible, with the result that it was possible to install only two torpedo tubes.

Was used diesel engine MWM RS-348, already in use aboard the Type IX-D; the electric motor was instead a AEG OJ 4463/8, a simplified version of the electric motors used in the type VII.

Seven Type XXIII were sunk before reaching the state of full operation:

- U-2331 - October 10, 1944, passed away in the Baltic Sea; unknown cause
- U-2342-26 December 1944 struck by a mine in the Baltic
- U-2344 - February 18, 1945, sank after colliding with U-2366 in the Baltic Sea
- U-2359-12 May 1945-sunk by British aircraft in the Kattegat
- U-2338-4 May 1945 sunk by British aircraft in the Baltic
- U-2367-5 May 1945 sank after colliding with another U-Boot in the Green Belt
- U-2365-5 May 1945 sunk by British aircraft in the Kattegat

Thirty-one were sunk at the end of the war, twenty surrendered to the Allies, and only three survived the war (the U-2326, U-2353 and U-4706).

The U-2336 sank the 2,300 tons of Avondale Park May 7, 1945, the last enemy sunk during the Battle of the Atlantic.

- Displacement: 234 tons (surfaced), 275 tons (submerged)
- Length: 34.7 meters Width: 3 meters Draft: 7.7 meters
- Gas Oil: 18 tons
- Speed: 9.7 knots (surfaced), 12.5 knots (submerged)
- Propulsion: 1 6-cylinder diesel engine from 575 hp MWM RS134S, 1 motor elttrico AEG GU4463-8 from 427 kW, 1 electric motor BBC CCR188 from 25.8 kW
- Batteries: 62 elements 2x21 MAL 740 (5,400 Amps)
- Autonomy: 4,450 miles nautical (6 knots surfaced) 2,600 miles nautical (8 knots surfaced), 194 miles nautical (4 knots submerged)

- Maximum depth: 180 meters
- Immersion time: 9 seconds
- Crew: 2 officers plus 12 crew members
- Armament: two torpedo tubes for two torpedoes from 533 mm with two torpedoes reserve

Axes U-boat of the Kriegsmarine

Otto Kretschmer

Ships sunk: 47
Tons sunk: 274,418 tons
Damaged ships: 5
Tons damaged: 37,965 tons

Commanded the boats U-35 (not in combat missions), U-23 (8 patrols) and U-99 (8 patrols).
The total includes 40 merchant ships sunk for a total of 208,954 tons, four warships sunk (the destroyer HMS Daring and three auxiliary cruisers, all British) for a total of 47,815 tons, a merchant ship captured by 2,136 tons, two merchant ships sunk but later recovered by the enemy for a total of 15,513 tons, and 5 merchant damaged for a total of 37,965 tons.
5 of sunken ships belonging to neutral nations.
Awarded the Knight's Cross of the Iron Cross with Oak fronds and Spade.

Wolfgang Lüth

Ships sunk: 47
Tons sunk: 225,756 tons
Damaged ships: 2
Tons damaged: 17,343 tons

Commanded the boats U-13 (not in combat missions), U-9 (6 patrols), U-138 (2 patrols), U-43 (5 patrols) and U-181 (2 patrols).
The total includes 46 merchant sunk for a total of 225,204 tonnes, a warship sunk (the French submarine Doris) of 552 tons, and two merchant ships damaged for a total of 17,343 tons.
5 of sunken ships belonging to neutral nations.
Awarded the Knight's Cross of the Iron Cross with Oak fronds, Swords and Diamonds (one of only two officers of the Kriegsmarine to get this honor).

Erich Topp

Ships sunk: 36
Tons sunk: 198,650 tons
Damaged ships: 4
Tons damaged: 32,317 tons

Commanded the boats U-57 (2 patrols), U-552 (10 patrols), U-3010 and U-2513 (the latter two not in combat missions).
The total includes 35 merchant sunk for a total of 197,460 tonnes, a warship sunk (the destroyer USS Reuben James) of 1,190 tons, and 4 for a total of 32,317 tons cargo damaged.
Two of sunken ships belonging to neutral nations.
Awarded the Knight's Cross of the Iron Cross with Oak fronds and Spade.

Günther Prien

Ships sunk: 31
Tons sunk: 191,919 tons
Ships damaged: 8
Tons damaged: 62,751 tons

Commanded only by boat U-47. The total includes 30 merchant sunk for a total of 162,769 tonnes, a warship sunk (the British battleship HMS Royal Oak) of 29,150 tons, and 8 for a total of 62,751 tons cargo damaged. 4 of sunken ships and damaged one of the ships belonging to neutral nations.
Awarded the Knight's Cross of the Iron Cross with Oak fronds.

Heinrich Liebe

Ships sunk: 34
Tons sunk: 187,267 tons
Ships damaged: 1
Tons damaged: 3,670 tons

Commanded the boats U-2 (not in combat missions) and U-38 (9 patrols). All ships were sunk or damaged cargo, and 10 of sunken ships belonging to neutral nations.
Awarded the Knight's Cross of the Iron Cross with Oak fronds.

Viktor Schütze

Ships sunk: 35
Tons sunk: 180,073 tons
Damaged ships: 2
Tons damaged: 14,213 tons

Commanded the boats U-19, U-11 (both not in combat missions), U-25 (3 patrols) and U-103 (4 patrols).
All ships were sunk or damaged cargo, and 5 of sunken ships belonging to neutral nations.
Awarded the Knight's Cross of the Iron Cross with Oak fronds.

Heinrich Lehmann-Willenbrock

Ships sunk: 25
Tons sunk: 179,125 tons
Damaged ships: 2
Tons damaged: 15,864 tons

Commanded the boats U-8 (not in combat missions), U-5 (1 patrol), U-96 (8 patrols) and U-256 (1 patrol).
The total includes 24 merchant sunk for a total of 170,237 tonnes, a merchant ship sunk by the enemy but recovered to 8,888 tons, and two merchant ships damaged for a total of 15,864 tons.
One of sunken ships belonged to a neutral country.
Awarded the Knight's Cross of the Iron Cross with Oak fronds.

Karl-Friedrich Merten

Ships sunk: 27
Tons sunk: 170,151 tons

Commanded only by boat U-68.
All were merchant ships sunk, no one belonging to neutral nations.
Awarded the Knight's Cross of the Iron Cross with Oak fronds.

Herbert Schultze

Ships sunk: 26
Tons sunk: 169,709 tons
Ships damaged: 1
Tons damaged: 9,456 tons

Commanded the boats U-2 (not in combat missions) and U-48 (8 patrols).
All ships were sunk or damaged cargo, and 4 of sunken ships belonging to neutral nations.
Awarded the Knight's Cross of the Iron Cross with Oak fronds.

Werner Henke

Ships sunk: 25
Tons sunk: 157,064 tons
Damaged ships: 2
Tons damaged: 7,954 tons

Commanded only by boat U-151.
The total includes 21 merchant sunk for a total of 131,769 tons, two warships sunk (an auxiliary cruiser and a seaplane British) for a total of 19,277 tons, a warship damaged (the British destroyer HMS Marne) of 1,920 tons, a merchant and a warship (a sloop British) sunk but recovered by the enemy for a total 6,018 tons, and a cargo of 6,034 tons damaged.
Awarded the Knight's Cross of the Iron Cross with Oak fronds.

Georg Lassen

Ships sunk: 26
Tons sunk: 156 082 tons
Damaged ships: 5
Tons damaged: 34,419 tons

Commanded the boats U-29 (not in combat missions) and U-160
(4 patrols).
All ships were sunk or damaged cargo, none of which belonging
to neutral nations.
Awarded the Knight's Cross of the Iron Cross with Oak fronds.

Joachim Schepke

Ships sunk: 37
Tons sunk: 155,882 tons
Damaged ships: 4
Tons damaged: 17,229 tons

Commanded the boats U-3 (3 patrols), U-19 (5 patrols) and U-100 (6 patrols).
The total includes 36 merchant sunk for a total of 153,677 tonnes, a merchant ship sunk by the enemy but recovered to 2,205 tons, and 4 for a total of 17,229 tons cargo damaged.
11 of sunken ships belonging to neutral nations.
Awarded the Knight's Cross of the Iron Cross with Oak fronds.

Heinrich Bleichrodt

Ships sunk: 25
Tons sunk: 152,320 tons
Damaged ships: 2
Tons damaged: 11,684 tons

Commanded the boats U-48 (2 patrols), U-67 (not in combat missions) and U-109 (6 patrols).
The total includes 24 merchant sunk for a total of 151,260 tonnes, a warship sunk (a sloop British) of 1,060 tons, and two merchant ships damaged for a total of 11,684 tons.
Awarded the Knight's Cross of the Iron Cross with Oak fronds.

Ernst Bauer

Ships sunk: 26
Tons sunk: 119,010 tons
Damaged ships: 4
Tons damaged: 31,304 tons

Commanded the boats U-120 (not in combat missions) and U-126 (5 patrols). The total includes 24 merchant sunk for a total of 111,564 tonnes, a warship sunk (a LCT British sunk with the ship carrying it) of 450 tons, a merchant ship sunk by the enemy but recovered to 6,996 tons, and damaged four merchant for a total of 31,304 tons.
Awarded the Knight's Cross of the Iron Cross.

Wilhelm Rollmann

Ships sunk: 25
Tons sunk: 103,884 tons

Commanded the boats U-34 (7 patrols), U-847 (not in combat missions) and U-848 (a patrol).
The total includes 20 merchant sunk for a total of 96,562 tons, two merchant ships captured totaling 4,957 tons, and three warships sunk (the cruiser minelayer Norwegian KNM Frøya, the British destroyer HMS Whirlwind, and the British submarine HMS Spearfish) for a total of 2,365 tons.
Six of the sunken ships (including both captured) belonged to neutral nations.
Awarded the Knight's Cross of the Iron Cross.

Made in the USA
Monee, IL
07 July 2026